Thomas Poppe

Espresso with the Devil

The Night he revealed his Tricks to me to Save the World

A Guide through Life's Labyrinths

Wisdom Keeper Publications

Wisdom Keeper Publications

https://wisdom-keeper.com
First published in German as "Espresso mit dem Teufel" by Irisiana, an Imprint of Penguin Random House 2021

Visit the author's website at:
www.paungger-poppe.com

ISBN: 9798708373977

Translation: Andreas Zantop & Thomas Poppe
Editorial: Corinne Attwood
Illustrations: Christian Martin Weiss
Cover Motive: © GettyImages-157189164 / elkor

Dear Reader,

Perhaps you are standing in your favorite bookstore right now, in a library, perhaps you briefly stopped at "Books and Magazines" in a train station or airport … and you wonder whether this book would be of any value for you.

Open it quickly anywhere, read two, three, four lines.

If these lines give you something right away, then this book is for you. If these lines shock you, worry you, annoy you – then all the more so.

We wish you many interesting insights and much luck and love on your path in life. May curiosity never leave you.

Tom and Fred

Fred´s Table of Contents

When I had already finished the manuscript for this book, a letter arrived without return address - a message from Fred:

My friend, remember, we did talk about this: you people tend to turn almost any activity into a habit. I took a leap of faith and quickly made a small table of contents to accommodate your "reading habits". I only ask your readers not to neglect the other topics when looking up a specific one. We have a mission!

Who am I to argue with Fred about such things, so I've added the listing here without comment.

Good evening. Please allow me to introduce myself: I am the Devil, but please call me Fred. No need to guess my name …

With these words, in perfect English and with the hint of a smile, the man stretches out his hand out. Automatically, I seize it, shaking it briefly. A firm handshake, a warm, dry hand. "Good evening. Please allow me to introduce myself: I am the Devil, but please call me Fred. No need to guess my name …"

The words of a stranger addressing me from the subdued lighting, in the middle of the night, at the bar of an airport hotel in the western USA. Words from "Sympathy for the Devil" by the Rolling Stones.
I notice that the hairs on the back of my right hand are tingling, standing up straight. A feeling creeps over me, I don't have a name for it ...

It is three o'clock in the morning, I've disembarked from a long flight from the southern tip of South America, and I'm waiting for the connecting flight to Europe. A double espresso is preventing me from slipping off the bar stool. A shower would be bliss, maybe also an upgrade to the reclining seats of first class … But no, spartan economy class awaits me on the plane. Quickly book a hotel room? No, it's not worth it anymore, a small screen between the whiskey bottles is showing the boarding and departure times ... and the devil is talking to me …

The man has an interesting face, he's wide awake, dressed casually and elegantly, with short, jet black hair, slightly graying here and there; I would probably buy a used car from him without bargaining. My eyes wander to the empty espresso cup in front of me. I am now certain that I've misheard – just as my counterpart continues to talk …

Excuse me for addressing you so directly, but a good conversation cuts the waiting time. However, if you want me to leave you alone, I'll understand. I always sympathize with … *someone's need for rest.*

The man draws out the last words, smiling at the same time. What does he want to tell me? Suddenly I'm not tired any more. Curious by nature, I think playing the game could be quite amusing.

No, you're right, that's my experience as well.

Wonderful. By the way, I've been looking for you. You are a writer, right?

For some reason, words tumble out of my mouth now as if I had been condemned to silence for years, and now I'm allowed to speak for the first time. Strange …

Right, how did you know? Are you familiar with my books? My face rarely appears in the media.

You've been looking for me? Why?
And why do you say that you're the "devil"?

Please take my word for it, that is very important tonight! Well, I'm not *a* devil. I am *the* devil.

Fred, the devil. Alright, Fred, I'll play along for now. My name is Thomas, but you can call me Tom. What springs to mind right away is that I actually imagine the "devil" to be something completely different, or someone completely different. You don't come even close to the images of you in my mind.

Instead of answering immediately, Fred smiles and pulls out a long, dark brown cigarillo from the inside pocket of his jacket. Snapping with the middle finger and thumb of his right hand, a small blue flame starts to flicker from the tip of his thumb. Slowly, he moves the flame to the tip of the cigarillo, lights it, extinguishes the flame with the thumb and index finger of his left hand, draws slowly on the cigarillo, and in exhaling blows an artful, bright red smoke curl into the air. Slowly, it expands, transforms into a three-

dimensional red heart and then dissolves in the draught of the air conditioner. As I stare at the smoke my breath is taken away for a moment – and Fred continues talking as if nothing had happened.

Tom, if the smoke bothers you, just tell me: times have changed a lot, indeed. Well, it's understandable, your point of view with regard to the alleged nature of the devil. That just shows me how good I was. My work in this world requires invisibility. Me and my merry men, we work *undercover* almost without exception. Believe me, hardly anyone suspects how and where I work most successfully. That was part of our craft. Until today … What do you think, how can you recognize a good secret agent?

If you ask me, you wouldn't recognize him at all.

Well said! That's a basic requirement for my task. Because those who recognize me have often escaped at that very second, at least for the time being. I can only shout after him: "See you next time!"
Are you okay? You look a little pale.

I'm fine, it's just lack of oxygen perhaps. Good. Alright, Fred, you're right, such a conversation between the worlds can sometimes change lives, I've experienced that myself. Sometimes one single

sentence is sufficient. Once, when I took a trip from the cool interior of Argentina to the scorching hot and humid Buenos Aires, I sighed audibly as I got off the charter bus: "If I'd known in advance it would be like this, I would've stayed on the farm." Which prompted a very sweet elderly lady in front of me to turn around and say serenely: "Oh come on, sweetheart, if you had known before, you wouldn't have been born." I've never forgotten that sentence.
So then, what leads the devil here to this place, on this beautiful night, to an airport in the middle of nowhere?

I want to talk to you.

To me? Is my time up already?

Don't worry, you haven't been on our list for quite some time. We can't be everywhere at once, that's why we only work on difficult cases which we have to work on continuously and intensively.
Those we do not consider to be a target any longer, we either have them in the bag, or they are no longer worth the trouble because they have *chosen* the right path – like you, for example.

> *The word "chosen" was emphasized by my interlocutor in an uncanny way, which sent a light, yet not unpleasant shiver down my spine. I made a mental note.*

With people like you, our rules of procedure only require that we prevaricate from time to time, sending one or two temptations so that you don't lose direction. You know, take Job from the Bible, and so on.
But you, my friend, you are a special case. And that's why I am seeking a dialogue with you tonight. Because you could be a great help to me. I would like you to record our conversation word for word and then distribute it all over the world – to the very last corner, if possible.

I'm supposed to help the devil? I'm afraid that could hurt my reputation …

I can't really grasp what makes me do it, but I press the audio recording button on my cell phone. What a strange guy ...

Yes, that would be my wish. And of course, I understand your concerns. But one question here: can you tell me in a few words what is your basic intention as a writer? What do you want your readers to gain from reading your works?

Maybe I sound a little pathetic now, but I want to give all readers useful tools to create a better world, both in the present and in the long term. And in all familiar areas of life – from sensible healthcare to environmentally friendly methods of construction and repair, all the way to successful organic farming and ... Wait, didn't you say you know my books? Then you're familiar with my aims. Reading my works is supposed to lead to more independence – and to a gradual turnaround towards harmonious cooperation between man and nature.

Let me hereby affirm that the two of us want the same, we are heading in the same direction. You have good intentions – and today *I* am dependent on you being successful with your good intentions.

In fact, we both have *the same* challenges and could perhaps solve them together. For that purpose, you would have to bring our conversation to the awareness of your readers. You shouldn't have a problem in finding channels for that, because there are already so many books about conversations with God, with Buddy, with her friends, with the Masters and Angels, and so on – I believe a dialogue between the two of us would certainly be of interest. As they say in your circles: *Audiatur et altera pars.*

It was about forty-five years ago that I had last heard Fred's last sentence. A teacher at my grammar school at that time refused to join in the prejudgment of a student who had been accused of a rather serious prank. Fact of the matter was that no other student was thought capable at that time of dropping a genuine, almost still warm cowpat on the principal´s desk, with a swastika engraved on top of it – definitely to hint at the undisputed Nazi past of the headmaster. Nobody gave my classmate the opportunity to defend himself; perhaps because he himself didn't even bother to. "Audiatur et altera pars" – "Let the other side be heard as well". This dictum of the old Roman legal system was quoted by my old Latin teacher, and he kept probing until the accused could prove a convincing alibi. Small wonder, because it was me *who'd put the cowpat there. I thought I could get away with it because no one would believe my having the audacity to do that, after nearly nine years of climbing through the grades with a "clean sheet". In fact, the authorship of this successful prank remained open back then. As if Fred was aware I'd come to the end of the foray through my memories, he resumed his talk.*

Good, for the time being, you should bear one thing in mind and think about it a little: from the beginning of time until today and into all eternity – *nothing ever happens without me!* Your countless conversations with Buddy and her Faithfuls, all those countless books and essays – none of them would make sense if I didn't exist.

The law of nature is that the good guys do not exist without the bad guys, winners would not have a chance if there were no losers, Yin is just hot air without Yang, any effort to improve and develop would be pointless because it would be *without exertion*, the Big Bang would not exist, many Nobel Prize winners would look pathetic without their wives …

Pardon me?

Just a joke, just a joke! Or rather, this is a special topic that we should perhaps touch on later. No, what I'm getting at is this: the earth would not exist if there were neither challenge nor incentive nor resistance to self-development. The mountaineer´s best friend is not only his ambition but also the mountain.

As far as the Nobel Prize winners are concerned, I agree with you wholeheartedly. Personality cult in any form is abhorrent to me. Role models, idols – I have no use for them. At least that's the way it is today. Even the most objective and factual acknowledgments, credits and award ceremonies can't change my mind. In the past, when I was younger, it was different, but in retrospect I have to say: actually, lifting people onto pedestals has always brought me nothing but disappointment. Except perhaps Beethoven, the Beatles and the Animal Liberation Orchestra. Do you know the band?

You can't argue about taste in music.

Okay, Fred, so: let's suppose you really are the devil. Well, my first question is: Why do you exist? What exactly is your task on this beautiful planet? To put obstacles in people's ways? Spread temptations? Promote greed, hate, envy? Run "Hotel Hell" in the underworld for the bad guys …? Your reputation is, as I said, truly nothing to brag about.

I can assure you, I am he. And what you are listing there – greed, hate, envy – that's for beginners; for that, I send out clueless apprentices from our ranks. That's how obviously destructive these things are. And "Hotel Hell"? Let's save that for later.
My miserable image is, in nearly all its aspects, my own work – a "red herring", a diversionary maneuver through all times and ages. As I said, in this way I could and can pursue my actual work undisturbed, because almost the whole world suspects me to be where I am not. When people saw the first train in history lurching toward them at 15 mph, hissing and puffing, they yelled: "The devil himself is haunting us!" – and they took off in all directions. We had a really good laugh back then, believe me.
So, you have my word: almost every time one of you preaches or mumbles fearfully: "That is devil's work!", or when someone paints a super scary image of an "underworld" with brush, idea or word, then it was me

who put about this conviction and let it mature into a fixed idea, an obsession – so as to bring my actual work to complete fruition, undiscovered.

My thoughts exactly! Whoever threatens you with the "devil's wrath" needs help or therapy to get rid of his anxieties – or his fanaticism, which is the same if you ask me. You should simply ignore such conduct, particularly on the part of the media! And above all, these people should not be elected into any kind of office! So, if all this "devil's work" is a distraction, what do you do all day long as secret agent of the underworld, if I may ask?

My tasks can be summed up in a few simple sentences. Let me start this way: I work day and night to convince people that comfort and convenience are their birthright. That standstill is more desirable than movement – physically, mentally and spiritually. I'm the inventor of the "Mañana Dictum": "Today can wait, tomorrow's another day!"

You did that? This dictum I know inside out! But what is there to do, after all? I always assumed that the inclination to idleness is an innate human trait you have to resist resolutely. That's what self-discipline was invented for. At least that's what they say …

Open your eyes, my friend. Have you ever watched a children's playground in the sunshine in spring? Being lazy is not in your nature at all, but the symptom of a certain condition. It only prevails when body, mind and soul no longer dance in sync towards a common goal but instead turn against each other. Body and mind in mutual dispute or conflict wastes more energy, more life-force than you can imagine. This is probably most evident in the first grades of your elementary schools. Watch how the children's bodies would much rather run across the meadows than have to spend hours on unnaturally shaped, cold seating furniture.

I remember my own school days, and you're right: I believe that if our gym teacher hadn't been convinced of the need for unconstrained playful movement at that time, my grades would've prevented me from attending high school.
*But sometimes you have to take a rest and indulge in idleness, righ*t?

The inertia and lethargy I'm talking about is the exact opposite of joyful and essential leisure and restoration. Truly successful people even master the art of relaxing from one creative work by engaging in another. But that's only one aspect of the story. You have to understand why I was so interested in promoting the pursuit of a comfortable life. Because I had my eye on the next step.
For that you have to keep in mind: standing still, stagnation, doing nothing – that actually doesn't exist at all! It is an illusion. What you allow something to stand

still, what you don't actively use, you condemn to another form of movement, namely, to the *activity of deterioration.* It dwindles and decays in the course of time which, of course, is also a form of movement.
Downwards, so to speak.
This holds true for muscles as well as for thinking, feelings, and intuition. Whoever strives for ease and convenience as a commodity or good, pays for it with decay – he betrays his dreams, the real tasks for which he or she came to earth in the first place.
Your scientists claim that the ability to read thoughts, telepathy, doesn't exist. This is something you can only establish with authority after you have let your sixth sense degenerate and replaced it with the Internet and phone, Google and Wikipedia which, on top of that, sell you convenient pseudo knowledge. Your deeper brain faculties fall asleep so that you don't even know the phone numbers of your loved ones by heart. Why do you think that in the year 1743 AC a midwife woke up at four o'clock in the morning, got dressed and rowed a mile across a lake because she knew that, over there, the fisherman's wife was about to give birth to a child? Do you think her cell phone had rung?

Well, looking at it that way …

Exactly! So: putting on brakes and *standstill,* that's my job. If you rest you rust, and rust is cool – in the eyes of the devil! Okay, now imagine you are physically fit and adventurous and decide to run the next New York marathon even though you have never jogged more than three miles in one go. Now suppose you give it a try and run a whole trial marathon without any problems. You feel fit at the end and don't even get out of breath, you don't have blisters on your feet, you hardly had to exert yourself … Just meditate on this picture for a moment.

But that would be no achievement at all! Where's the joy of succeeding in that?

Another example: imagine you want to learn to play the guitar - you grab the instrument, and the very next day you're already playing like Eric Clapton. What's wrong with this picture?

I think I understand …

Anyone who is seduced by my inducements to laziness and standstill, I have in my bag. On the other hand, those people who never want to stop learning, they are my natural targets. Whoever is curious without prejudice, I have to pay special attention to.

Seems to me that the number of your victims is not exactly small.

Correct, actually I should've insisted on being paid per person. Joking aside: encouraging standstill, playing the brakeman, has many side effects and ramifications, as you will see. So I seduced you into declaring your currently cultivated opinions, convictions, and beliefs as "truth" that no longer needs to be examined. That is convenient and gives you a deceptive feeling of security. Fake News was my best helper here because a lie usually takes root in the mind much faster than the truth. "Give a rumor a few hours head start, and the whole world knows about it." Just one of your wise sayings. This holds especially true when the falsehood reinforces a prejudice. If I was successful here, I naturally also brought about standstill and mental deterioration.

You've just pressed a big fat button in my mind! If I were education secretary anywhere in the world I would introduce "Plausibility" or "Fact Checking" as a mandatory subject! Maybe even "Body Language as a means to detect lying"! "How do I distinguish media truth from media lies?", or "How do I spot a fake statistic?". And I would do anything to stop "deep fakes" and to prosecute and punish Internet trolls! Those are criminals that can change a person's life, throw them completely off their tracks.

Good thought. But as long as you keep on electing politicians who only have your welfare in mind – if at all

– a few weeks before an election, then nothing will come of it.
Okay, what happens when people cling to their convictions like drowning people clutch at the proverbial straw?

Well, everything that looks like real discourse and discussion, a friendly exchange of experiences, synergy, compromise – that disappears from everyday life. You can watch that unfolding every single day in the news …

Right. Wherever true togetherness, harmony and balance prevail or are striven for, rivalry and envy creep out of all cracks and holes. *That* was my job. I pushed people apart. And in the next step: wherever you fought something or someone directly, there I was, cheering you on. Because only very few of you understand that fighting a thing or person does not weaken it, but only strengthens it. But we'll get back to this later in more detail.
My biggest adversary here has always been your strong sense of the value of harmony and togetherness, and the equality of all people, which is anchored in your souls. If you were to give this particular feeling, this *knowledge*, a chance in your life, it could actually make you immune to my temptations. But for the moment, in summary: **I made standstill, opposition and black-and-white thinking attractive and helped to make impartial**

curiosity an alien concept for you. And believe me, my tools for achieving this goal have always been up to date and very efficient.

Comfort and convenience more tempting than pulling yourself together? Competitive thinking and rivalry? Goodness me, your blandishments beam at us from every billboard and make up 80 per cent of a normal TV show! Whole industries do your groundwork! Everywhere we get to hear directly or subliminally: "The way you are, you're not good enough. Be more, be richer, be faster, owning five cars is more moral than owning just four, better to fly seven thousand miles on vacation than to take a bike ride in the countryside outside the city!" Everywhere you look, it's a rat race. Stress wherever we turn our eyes! Even the corona virus hasn't changed the situation that much.
But there's a contradiction here: after all, there is hectic movement everywhere as well, striving for "progress", the ideology of growth at any price?

No contradiction. Here, the stasis is inward, reinforcing artificial ideologies as meaningful and perhaps even natural. Your ideology of constant growth in the economy, for example, is sheer, absolute, utter insanity.

Yes, and the few voices of reason find themselves exposed to contempt, hate speech and pitfalls. They've even turned the expression "do-gooder" into a swear word to describe them.

Right, the amount of money we spend on TV commercials is almost as high as the worldwide military spending we inspired. And what did we advertise on our posters primarily? Well, exactly what "convenience" promises – products that relieve you of the effort of exercising the body, exercising the mind, exercising your spirit, real and in depth understanding of a problem, and above all: *thinking things through to the end* – that should be one of your principal capabilities. If you want to neutralize my work of destruction, you must make it your number one priority to regain and further develop this ability.

"Thinking things through to the end"? What do you mean exactly?

It means to look calmly at something - a problem, an obstruction - with many pairs of eyes and from all sides; to find out its real origin, the real causes, and work out promising and achievable strategies for the future. And it means to look closely at the consequences of one's actions. Where does the billiard ball roll, what does the seventh move in the chess game look like? It means to assess all the available and also the impossible paths until one arrives at a result, at a decision. And only then to give the green light for action. Thanks to me, you have forgotten how to engage in thinking things through to the end. Otherwise there would be no nuclear power plants.

Exactly! How can we bequeath to our children waste that will still be polluting the planet 300,000 years from now! And even brainwash them into believing our justifications for it! Thinking things through to the end should be a mandatory subject in every high school – no, it should be practiced already in Kindergarten!

Well, with my active help you have learned to consider the development from bicycles to self-driving cars as "progress"; from the glass of water that eliminates headaches in 29 minutes to the aspirin that stifles headaches in 28 minutes, but does not eliminate them. You have almost completely lost sight of what all this time saving and convenience is meant to achieve – what is the real goal of this journey? The more time you save, the less you have any idea of how to use the time saved in a fruitful way.

Correct too! We produce things that seem to do everything better than humans, without asking, now what? The assistance systems in cars will sooner or later make driver's licenses obsolete. We invent prosthetic devices and crutches for all human abilities. And then we are surprised when these abilities are lost. Kids today can't even read maps anymore! Seems to me the amount of time saved increases just as quickly as the general stress level.

I've blinded you to the fact that stress occurs only when one of two conditions are met: acting "yes" and thinking "no", or acting "no" and thinking "yes". Whoever understands this will never have to suffer from stress again. There is a world of difference between joyful exertion and stress. To have swept this truth under the table – that is one of my masterpieces.

But I give you credit for the fact that I have worked very quietly and unobtrusively. For example, if there was a choice between an escalator and a staircase, we were always there to recommend the escalator. Fitness freaks who were resolutely heading for the stairs, we quickly whispered in their ears: "Just this one time …" "Once is as good as never", that saying is also one of mine. Clever, isn't it?

You're an anti-stair climber? Orthopedists, actually the entire medical profession, should be particularly pleased with your work.

Well observed. When someone makes twenty times more money than the person who produces the food on his table, we usually have very little work to do; these people are already where we want them to be.

What do you mean by that?

Come on, use your brain, my friend.

I'm supposed to figure it out for myself ... ? At the moment, all I can think of is my observation that wealth does not change people, it merely reveals how they really are.

You are getting closer ...

Stop - before I get too sidetracked, can we please talk about what´s been on the tip of my tongue for quite some time already? You say you chose me because I'm a writer. But that doesn't explain why I should publish our conversation!
Betraying your trade secrets – that just cannot be in your best interests if the secret of your success is working behind the scenes. Why play hide and seek for so many thousands of years, and then suddenly put your cards on the table? Fred, you must explain that!

> *I get the clear feeling that I already know Fred well. I don't know from where, when and under what circumstances, but the longer he talks, the more certain I am. The choice of words, the intonation –the man is part of my past!*

Why hide for centuries or even thousands of years, and then come out right here and now?

Thousands of years? Tom, my friend, I was there right from the very beginning, the very first moment. But of course you're right, I have to explain why I want to put

my cards on the table now. There are two reasons for that: you should write everything down, word for word, and make it accessible, word for word, to all people, if possible in all languages.
The thing is this, and herein lies the plight that has led me to you:
The devil is a workaholic!
In action around the clock, seven days a week!
I am at work! And I enjoy it!
I hate idleness! I don't need a vacation!

Yeah, alright, alright, but so what? What's the problem? Just one glance at any daily newspaper in any country in the world is enough to prove that you're not only having fun; you're also extremely successful.

But that's exactly the problem! I was *so* successful that you people are now well on the way to kicking me into unemployment for a very long time! Higher, faster, farther, richer! This path has brought you to the edge of the abyss.
You're just about to completely eliminate yourselves from this beautiful planet for the thirty-eighth time since the last Great Exhalation! Since the "Big Bang", as you call it …

Fred, you can't scare me, tell me something new. The little bit of common sense I've managed to acquire tells me that you´re right.

Nevertheless, out of the devil's mouth … Pardon the irony: if we jump over the cliff, wouldn't it be just what you intended for us? That's what you've worked for, damn it, you would have deserved that reward!

No! … Yes! … No! … For Buddy´s sake, of course I see what you're saying! You're right, my main goal was to be the great brake, to bring you to a standstill, to routine and to sleep, but that's just a game in the grand scheme of things in the universe!

You are not in this world to hand me the final victory!

You are not in this world to pilot this magnificent playground called earth towards destruction - just because the false pride and the childish games of your politicians and the antagonisms of the world feel like an "innate part of human nature"!

You even went so far to invent the madness of "might is right" or the imagined law of the "survival of the fittest", all without my help! You have to wake up now! What does a school class gain by blowing up the school? What does the marathon runner win when the first blister on his foot "inspires" him to stop?

My goodness, now what is your problem really? Sounds to me like a very rarified complaint! That can't be it!

It may sound like a luxury problem in your ears, but I assure you it is not. My dilemma can be put quite simply: *You are making it too easy for me!*
Every time you blow yourself up and out of this wonderful paradise called earth, a long break awaits me during which I more or less just twiddle my thumbs and watch reruns of old movies with Buddy and my friends. In the meantime, the planet gives itself a few hundred thousand years of your calendar to recover from you.
Of course, even then I don't run out of work, because Earth is not my only sphere of duty, but my job is not to be so successful that you render this wonderful elite university called earth uninhabitable in record time!
And later, when everything starts all over again with Stone Age number thirty-nine: the constant struggle for bare survival gives you a lot of instructive experiences, but to be an A+ student and have to repeat the same grade can be terribly boring, after all!

No doubt about it. But okay, what is my job now? After all, what can I do about it, really? How is a single book supposed to put a stop to this process?

You are just perfect for the job! No sweet-talk here, but your ego has just the perfect size. Small enough not to lose sight of the actual task and remain objective, yet large enough to deal with the ensuing publicity.

Watch out for one thing though: don't try to justify yourself or prove anything. This book will draw its energy from the fact that every reader, drawing on his or her own inner resources, will derive benefit from it and find his or her own way back to the essentials in life. Because only then will the new way have substance and resilience, and people become immune to criticism and hostility.

Hmmm, that's already the first stumbling block, because I can write reasonably well when holed up somewhere in peace and quiet, but in public there is no time to weigh my words; I string words together in haste, and often notice too late that they could be misconstrued. And then instant self-criticism clogs my grey cells …

No problem, just stick to the rule of not trying to persuade anyone or anything, and take your time with the answers. Stick to what you know, and if you don't know the answer just say so. People will have your back to stop the army of arsonists And you've already proved that you can resist the temptation to become a guru. The gist of the matter is: yes, it can succeed if, in the future, my work on earth becomes visible to every human being. Those who recognize me find it easier to say "No" to me. All they need is trust in their own free will.

The opportunity already exists. You would find enough supporters for the good cause, and not just among Greenpeace members. Greta Thunberg is not alone! Yes, and Mama Buddy would be the one most pleased. So, do I have you on board?

Without a moment's hesitation! You didn't choose me at random though, did you? So, by the way, who is "Mama Buddy"?

Buddy? Oh, I forgot to explain. That's insider jargon. Mama (or Papa) Buddy is our nickname for the "Best Friend in the Universe Forever and Ever". That's the lady or gentleman you have given various names in the past: God, Buddha, Gaia, Allah, Krishna, Manitou, Odin, Great Spirit, Mother Nature, etc. Of course, these names were not important, only the being, the power which was so named, that was and is important. Among ourselves, we just call it Buddy. Buddy is short, Buddy sounds cool, and Mama Buddy herself, she likes it too. ***It was Buddy who set me on my mission.***

Buddy. Sounds good. Hey, so the Lord's Prayer should start with "Best friend in Heaven" or "Buddy in Heaven" … Somehow catchy …

That's the spirit!

Hold on! You just said Buddy set you on your mission! So the devil is sent by God …?

Sent the very second Buddy conceived this universe. I am the counterweight, the balance, the darkness without which you can't even recognize light. The effort before the joy. The sweet after the bitter. The weight on the swift foot. The fever that makes the sick person start to appreciate good health.

That's a lot of food for thought …

That's the purpose of our meeting here. One more thing: I've prepared some additional texts and tricks – let's call them "hacks" – for you that will help your readers steer their current situation in a positive direction by their own efforts. I recommend that you distribute them throughout your book intuitively and as you see fit. These are words from the mouths of people who have become immune to my temptations, and who in turn have snatched many of you away from my influence. Pioneers for the good cause, so to speak.

> *Fred hands me a thin folder which I open briefly and skim through its pages. It contains texts and short quotations. I've distributed them uncensored and according to my gut feeling on the following pages.*

Okay, but that's quite a few … and on glancing through here they deal with very diverse topics. Don't you think the structure of the book will get a bit chaotic?

My goodness, don't worry, we can dip in at will. This will not be a linear textbook with lessons one through ten. By the way, do you happen to have heard of one of the most important books in all of history? It's called "Fihi ma Fihi", written in Arabic by a guy called Rumi in the thirteenth century of your calendar. Translated into English, the title means: "It is in it what is in it". It was written with the author´s awareness that every reader will get out of the book what he or she is ready for at the time, depending on his or her ability to understand. And of course, depending on their level of courage, I'd like to add. We will work in the same way - what do you think? Your book will pick up everyone at his or her own level, like a good teacher would.

Perhaps it might be a good idea to tell your readers to treat it somewhat like a divinatory book. Just open it up at random from time to time and start reading. That produces the greatest benefit.

So may I summarize? I'm supposed to do industrial espionage in the underworld, but with the knowledge and approval of the boss of the underworld. Interesting job. And what's the second reason for our meeting? Earlier you said there were two …

The second reason? Oh yes, that might sound a bit trivial. Even I need an opportunity from time to time to express myself. A casual chat here and there – and my task is no longer so … how should I say … dark? My job can be lonely at times.
So, you have to help people get to know me. As long as you see me and my task as something that has to be opposed with all your might, or that you have to be scared of, you can't *understand* my work here. Only someone who understands can act correctly. Blind opposition makes me stronger, whereas understanding enables you to see through me and to decide and act for the good. You won't get a single step closer to your goal if you believe that you first have to identify and find all the "wrong ways".

Alright, no problem, we're talking to each other now. So tell me how you work – and what I'm supposed to do? Making your methods public might not be enough. Hopefully you'll also tell me how to avoid your pitfalls and seductions.

Exactly! That's my intention. "Devil hacks"! This folder here contains some very effective ones, and together we´ll present quite a few more.

What's a "devil hack"?

Yes, "hack", that's an expression kids use nowadays for what used to be called simply a trick or knack. My people invented the label "Devil Hack" whenever one of you found a way to make yourself immune to us.
An example? Recently, one of my faithful disciples decided to end the ongoing feud with his neighbor, and to calmly endure his ridicule for turning his English lawn into a chaotic flowering haven for bees. Serenity and tolerance were his "devil hacks" – and right then and there he was able to distance himself from my blandishments.
Elsewhere on earth, a Christian missionary abruptly stopped preaching and brainwashing people because he suddenly had a flash of realization - it would be enough to simply exemplify and live his faith in order to successfully convey its meaning and value to people. His devil hack was common sense and unconditional human love. And of course the realization that, up to that point, he had preached water, yet drunk wine. The

fact that he was summarily excommunicated opened his eyes even further and made him even more successful in his endeavors. Or look at yourself: do you recall a sudden realization that anger and rage arise from disappointed personal expectations – and are thus self-made?

My goodness, yes! I remember! At that time I was twenty, and I'd grabbed a book in a bookstore with the title "Think on these Things" and opened it exactly on that page ...
Now I understand: a devil hack is a tool to resist your temptations and steer the world and/ or yourself onto a better path. Devil hack sounds fitting.

Good, let's stick to that.

Whatever I do not use and care for, degenerates. My six senses, which I do not care for or cultivate through use and sharpening, make me blind, deaf and dumb. Love, which I do not cultivate by unconditionally showing and giving, makes me lonely and makes me perish. (The Translator)

Okay, back to the essentials: I'm supposed to write about our conversation? And I'm supposed to help ruin your work …

No! Not only "about", the *whole* conversation please! Unabridged! Add nothing, leave nothing out. After all, you've always been past masters at distorting, lying and producing fake news, I didn't have to teach you anything at all in that respect. Therefore, in this case, my plea for accuracy and care. The entire conversation, the whole kit and caboodle …

Good, that makes it easy, and I'll do my best. I've already clicked "record" on my cell phone to be on the safe side. Agreed?

Sure! And please forgive me if it doesn't turn into a real conversation or dialogue. I'm a telegram carrier, not a discussion partner.

> *Dear readers, at this point please don't entertain the idea that one day there will be a podcast or audio file of this conversation. After I'd transcribed it word for word, it disappeared from my cell phone. And I assure you that I did not accidentally press the "delete" button!*

That's okay, I've had some practice in listening. But before I forget –you mentioned the Big Bang earlier. I'm curious: did it really happen?

Yes and no – well, it's actually quite simple: that is the moment when Buddy changes from inhaling to exhaling again. In this sense, the Big Bang is not a unique event. Eternity is real, you see.

By the way, since you mentioned it: "Our Father in Heaven", this line was a brainwave of one of my staff members, because it helped conceal two vital truths: firstly, that Buddy is neither female nor male. More about that later, if we have some time left. And secondly, that Buddy does not live somewhere "up there" in a heavenly realm but rather is closer to you than the tip of your nose – and that's twenty-four hours a day, seven days a week. Can you see the inescapable conclusion?

Right now words elude me …

Well, that's understandable, considering what I've been forever drumming into you. So, it follows that, from the beginning of time until this very moment, there was never a real *need for mediators* between Buddy and each and every one of you, without exception.
What is true, however, is that at all times there has been a need for certain humans acting as *signposts. And there was never a lack of those, believe it or not!* They have been at your service at all times in history – with the exception perhaps of a few years in the time you call the Middle

Ages. But you either ignored most of the guides or fed them to the lions, quartered them, burned them, and worse. In truth your strongest weapon against these good people was not the creation of martyrs, but something else. Can you guess what that is?

What could be worse than slaughtering them?

Simply ignoring them, and discounting them as successful and truthful guides.

I hardly dare think it, but are you saying that we don't really need priests at all, no Men of God? Maybe even no religion?

Well, guides and signposts are valuable assets, but firstly never as a fundamental requirement, and secondly only if they are *authentic* guides – and there are very few of those. And you certainly don't need anyone cracking the whip and brainwashing you with crackpot ideas such as "mortal sin", celibacy, the veiling requirement for women and other such nonsense.

Anyway, why mediators, you lazybones? Why are you so willing to fall for my temptations? There is not a hair's breadth of a gap between you and Buddy, not even here and now. This basic truth applies to all of you, no exceptions here. No one is rejected, no one is abandoned, no one is really alone, no mistake is so big that someone will be abandoned. If you seriously miss

Buddy and search for her, but you don't feel and hear her soft voice, then you certainly won't hear and feel her in a synagogue, mosque, temple or church. Any sense of distance, any feeling of abandonment, or deafness to Buddy´s voice, that's your own thinking and doing, your own responsibility, your own illusion which – I must confess – of course I supported as much as I could. I always suggested to you: "Better listen to the pastor or the imam than to your own feelings", and "Better twenty years with an entertaining guru than to open up to Buddy here and now." Sorry, but I was just being me, after all.

Whoever sleeps with the dogs,
wakes up with fleas.
Whoever brings roses
lets eyes sparkle.
The art of living also entails not being surprised
when we reap what we sow. (The Translator)

Sometimes even I am scared by how easy it was for me to do this to you. With open arms, you welcomed the loneliness and fear of life as an atheist – with the same enthusiasm as the constant stress and alienation from Buddy because of the imaginary fear of a punishing tyrant God.

Instead of thinking it through and arriving at the inescapable conclusion: Buddy would never come up with the idea of withdrawing from her children and thus punishing herself!

This is crucial, my friend: what your peddlers of religion have called and still call "God's punishment" is either the harvest of what you have sown yourself, or it is a chapter in a script that you chose of your own free will before you were born – as learning experience and challenge.

Before I was born?

That's how it is, but patience! I'll get to that in a minute. Think it over: if you're afraid of being "punished", separation and resistance and fear ensue, but very rarely insight. But if you called it "consequence of action" you would find a valid answer to these questions: "What is the cause? How can I improve things?" Ever heard of the term "Karma"?

Now I'm getting goosebumps because I've always thought or at least felt this way, but okay, I promise, I'll take notes, I'll record everything. And I won't ruminate or speculate too much now. So what else is part of your repertoire? Where are you at work? Where do we meet you in person?

So what to reveal next? Okay, perhaps this: part of our covert operations in recent centuries has been to promote professional specialization all over the world, and at the same time to make sure that the words "specialist" and "expert" were highly esteemed.

Now you'll have to explain that to me in more detail. Yes, I also have my experiences and reservations, but what in your opinion is wrong with specialists or experts?

Oh, nothing. Provided their work serves the genuine progress of the soul and the harmonious co-existence of all people as well as of man and nature. However, we built in a clever trap leading to specialization. The specialist focuses on the parts of a larger whole and then begins to "reside" in the parts, as it were. He explores all angles and aspects of his tiny field and gradually turns into an authority, perhaps even a beacon of his subject. We made sure that he or she is exposed to a form of permanent temptation, and we were very satisfied with the results. What do you think that could have been?

Sorry, I can't think of anything other than becoming an authority is an ideal way of inflating the ego. I've been able to observe this temptation in myself quite well. And of course, it leads to all kinds of disadvantages for the person and his associates. The "Gods in White Coats" in the medical profession, and so on ...

Right, vanity makes blind. But there is something else: in the work of the specialist the whole behind the part undergoes a transformation. The true interconnectedness of a problem, an illness, a disturbance gradually degenerates into a side issue, a minor matter, yes, it even turns into an annoying obstacle. If you spend months tinkering with a defective spark plug, or even if your life's ambition is to develop the perfect spark plug, then over time you'll become less and less interested in where you originally wanted to go with your vehicle. Taken to the extreme, specialists are often like people who first want to analyze the composition of the smoke before they allow the fire department to put out the fire.

"Smoke catchers"?

Exactly – and where is this attitude most visible in everyday life?

In politics?

Close. In the current state of your healing arts. With my active assistance, you have transformed it into a symptom fighting machine. Your specialist doctors usually have very little idea what illness and what health

really mean, and what the deeper underlying causes of a physical disorder are. And these are almost always to be found in an imbalance within a whole. The actual cause can even be something minor like a disturbing modern art painting on your wall. It sends a stream of negative energy to the observer, which eventually results in physical illness. Much like living with a chronically depressed person in your home.
The gradual ignoring of real causes is spreading even in your psychological sciences. Or why do you think child psychologists only very rarely invite parents into therapy sessions? Or why today more and more therapists resort to chemicals to help the soul?

Until just very recently, your "World Health Organization" defined "health" officially, as if carved in stone, as the "absence of illness". Any questions? Want more examples?

50 per cent of all back pain is caused by stressed kidneys, and chocolate is a strong migraine trigger. Nevertheless, the internist and orthopedist do not talk to each other. And chocolate manufacturers as well as customers usually have no clue of the interconnections, because the headaches do not start until about twelve to twenty-four hours after consumption.

Now that you mention it: A chocolate bar in the evening, and I can hardly open my eyes the next morning!

Not just you. Eighty per cent of all physical illnesses have their real cause in your everyday "normal" diet. But not a single doctor is confronted with compulsory courses in "healthy nutrition" during his or her studies and practical semesters. If they look into it voluntarily, or study with nutrition experts, they'll be served "the latest science". With the guarantee that, after three months at the latest, another "up to date science" will be presented as "truth".

A pursuer of truth must not act out of consideration for customs. He must always be open to correction, and if he discovers that he is in error, he must, at all costs, admit it and make amends. (Mahatma Gandhi)

Take a close look: in your hospitals, the patients often get exactly the same food delivered to their bedside that made them sick in the first place. Another fact is: many doctors themselves would never take what they prescribe to their patients, if they were in the same situation. By the way, do you know who is responsible for the success of a cure?

I would have thought that was obvious, but now that you ask me, I have to reconsider. In my experience almost the entire human race believes it is a doctor or a healer.

It is always the sick person who heals himself. The art of a true healer consists in creating circumstances that allow your body, mind and soul to *remember* what health means. Having done so, body, mind and soul work together *as a team* and heal themselves. This is one of the greatest secrets of all healing arts, and all true healers take it to heart.

"Confessions of a Medical Heretic!" – that's one of the coolest books I've ever read. Written by a medical practitioner by the name of Robert Mendelsohn.

Hey, I know that man! Fortunately for many of you, I just couldn't shut him up. Yes, your tendency to focus on symptoms rather than causes made my job easy from the very start. You suppressed the most important thing from your consciousness and banished it into the basement, namely, that everything is connected to everything else. You cannot eradicate a species of insect on a South Sea island with pesticides without the consequences soon having a negative impact on Alaska. Truly, your artificial country borders and walls are sometimes a sad sight even for me, because there's not one genuine problem that would stop at a border. The fifteen thousand children that you let starve to death every day are a problem for all of you, not just for poor Third World countries that you have exploited. Not to mention global warming.
So many symptoms, so little insight! Brexit, for example, is such a foolish a signal to the world that it could have been my own work.

And I was a convinced until this moment that it was indeed your work! How else can a people let themselves be fooled like that! On the other hand, I admit that the EU, or rather the Brussels bureaucratic state, has made really stupid mistakes. For instance they could have made an effort to show British citizens how they benefitted from being in the EU - a small flyer would have sufficed…

No, indeed Brexit is your work, which is probably little comfort for you. So when a man who has long since eradicated all traces of empathy in himself shouts "America first!", he is like a spleen that yells "I am more important than all the other organs"!

But what about medical care, the fact that we are all now covered by health insurance, which is one of the greatest achievements of our civilization?

Basically correct, but not all of you have health insurance. Fifty million Americans, for example, cannot even afford to visit a doctor, let alone benefit from his or her diagnostic and therapeutic measures. Unfortunately, I've been all too successful in this area. My brainwashing succeeded in convincing your orthodox medical practitioners that raking in ten to a hundred times more money than a farmer or baker is well deserved and quite moral. Accordingly, they consider themselves to be more "valuable" than most of their fellow human beings.

Well, I was afraid you were behind this. To measure the value of a person by the size of his bank account - that could only have been you.

Your emergency medicine is okay, thanks to state-of-the-art machinery and aids. But the vast majority of doctors today are almost exclusively concerned with treating symptoms. Life is prolonged at all costs, even if the prolonged life no longer deserves to be called "life". You should take more responsibility for yourselves! Your doctors even prescribe antibiotics for common colds! Research into the real causes of illness yields too little money, and does not lead to Nobel Prizes. Comprehensive and, above all, comprehensible information and genuine, effective prevention have become uninteresting for you, as they do not result in huge revenue or impressive sales figures. "Let´s throw billions of dollars at it, and in twenty years' time, at the latest, we'll have found the cause of obesity in the genes."

Yes, of course, that would bring in a lot more money than simply stopping eating the wrong things. Just the other day I saw a TV commercial for a pill for heartburn. After the actors had popped it, you could see them happily shoveling in pizzas and burgers again, because "now nothing can hurt any longer". Back then, I thought that it was as if the pharmaceutical industry was selling pillows to people suffering from headaches because they were constantly hitting themselves on the head with a wooden mallet.

Yes, and that´s still not enough. You succeed in hindering the true healers, the born healers, for example, by only giving access to the medical profession to students who manage to adapt to an artificial and industry-friendly school curriculum – namely, the "straight A" students. Or to kids whose parents have the moolah. What do you think is the hallmark of a true healer?

Well, I think, whoever heals is right. And somehow I think … no, I'm absolutely convinced, that he or she must love people.

Right, a good doctor is first and foremost qualified by knowing and loving people and clearly feeling the calling to heal. What was it like with the "A" students you've met during your life? Would you describe them as "inherently qualified to be doctors"?

On the contrary. I just remember one of them - a master hair-splitter, arrogant, out of touch with life, never had a girlfriend until graduation day, always A+ in Math and Latin, but never helped us lowlifes with our homework. I later found out that he'd become a gynecologist.
I'm somewhat familiar with today's medical training. The system actively blocks the ability to heal and ensures that only the "right"

ones make it, those who later turn into good executives of the system. Worst of all in my opinion is that doctors today are required to follow strict and "standardized" protocols after diagnosis. Standardization! As if we were all identical machines. Individuality is abolished, which is sheer madness. Because what helps and heals one person is an additional burden for another. This requires experience and intuition!
It's the same in almost all schools, where the really good teachers have no chance of becoming principals or headmasters.

A fine devil hack at this point: **Take your time in peace and quiet to observe who, in your environment, gets the chance to become a role model and how the process unfolds.** You can learn a lot from that. After all, who in your country manages to appear on the pages and screens of the media? Is it the losers and winners of fights, or is it the silent heroes who prevent fights?

A recent quote from a television manager: ""As long as the gun is still smoking and hot…!"

That's right. You are served pictures of heroic firemen and law enforcement agents but not the much greater heroes who prevent fire and conflict. "**Outstanding doctors prevent diseases. Mediocre doctors take care of diseases that have not yet erupted.**

Insignificant doctors treat existing diseases." This saying is from ancient China.

The truth that frees us and
brings us forward
is almost always the truth
that we don't want to hear at first.
So when we say something is not true, we all too often mean: "I don't want to hear it". (The Translator)

I'll gladly pass on this saying!

Sorry, here's another case where I did a great job of confusing the issue and turning the truth on its head. A question to ponder: Who is the true hero? The psychotherapist who works for months and years to help nervous, moody, irritable "problem" children, who writes three books about his experiences, receiving worldwide attention and praise for them? Or is it the school director who only allows organic food without meat, dairy and eggs in his school cafeteria, who bans all sugar-contaminated soft drinks and sweets, so that none of his students need therapy any more, let alone long-term medication?

I always say: follow the money. Those who make money from sick people, what's their primary interest? The meat and dairy industry has a zillion times more money available for advertising than independent science, which has long since proved how unhealthy meat and dairy are. The money they've been given has come from the very same people they've made sick!

A simple devil hack here, too: **always observe who gives advice and why. What does he want to achieve with his advice? What has this person achieved by thinking and acting the way he thinks and acts? Observe and arrive at your own judgment. "By their fruits you shall know them."** One of my most important tasks was to take away your confidence to ask those questions. The Emperor's New Clothes are not supposed to be questioned.

Right, the saying about fruit has spared me more than one disappointment in life. Today I know that people should be judged not by their opinions but by what their opinions turn them into.

See? So you already know a few devil hacks, and that is a particularly good one, congratulations! Perhaps in the future you will also apply a law of nature that is not taught in any school: ***"No man can achieve health or success by moaning, and no problem can be solved, no illness can be cured, by fighting the problem or illness."***

No one can bring about lasting improvement if he does not convey the pleasure of it to all those involved. Whoever is constantly dealing with problems will always have them, and will even radiate them.

I've got an idea what the answer is, but I'll ask the question anyway: why should fighting an illness or a problem not lead to success?

Because only understanding a problem leads to success, to real solutions! Unfortunately, you have willingly accepted all my inducements and suggestions about "fighting instead of understanding". Wherever something or someone was being attacked, there I was, encouraging the fighters to the bitter end - which is ***no*** end! Consequently, you have slowly turned into firefighters who, when called to a blaze, as first emergency measure, set up huge smoke extraction systems and then celebrate that as a victory. And the media applaud, the spectators applaud.

A current example: fighting terrorists always generates new terrorism. Understanding terrorism, on the other hand, and recognizing its causes, is the *only* way to arrive at a solution. If an "eye for an eye" remains your principle, everyone will be blind in the end. The same applies to the fight against disease. Why do you think more and more bacteria are becoming immune to your antibiotics?

I've also noticed that since 9/11 there has not been a single article in the media that has seriously dealt with the causes of terrorism. Not even articles that asked the question about the causes. Quite the contrary: it seems that wanting to "understand" a terrorist is something bad or evil, is politically incorrect. Perish the thought that terrorism might be close to an inevitable and automatic reaction to suppression and exploitation!

Right – and as far as the true causes of illnesses are concerned: adequate health insurance in case of illness has a side effect I had planned for. Namely, that it has become much easier to relinquish self-responsibility and "call in sick". As a parallel consequence, when people get sick, you rarely come up with the best course of action, the only appropriate devil hack: "Where have I allowed an imbalance in my life, so that it manifests itself now in my illness? What does the disease want to tell me?" Instead, you take refuge in well-trodden paths: "Doctor, it is your job to cure me. Nothing else interests me." Note how strongly vested interests in medicine have suppressed the knowledge of the interconnection between body, mind and soul. Just fifty years ago, the term "psychosomatic medicine" was on everyone's lips.

Wow, that's right! Knowledge of the mutual influence of physical and mental states has been largely swept under the carpet; it doesn't appear in the media, let alone in schools. Look at the hidden disdain with which the medical profession uses the word "Placebo". "It is only a Placebo effect" As if it's something minor, negligible! They have the secret under their very noses!

And on top of that, illness and various ailments have become the only way for many people to get a minimum of attention and care. Your soul knows all too well that love and joy are the highest and best medicine. Lack of love and joy is at the root of almost every illness and disorder that can affect the body. Your daily malnutrition and inhumane working conditions are, strictly speaking, just symptoms of unkindness – of other people, employers, etc. towards each other and themselves.

Love your neighbor as yourself would be the primary devil hack here.

Concealing these intimate connections was my work as well. Right from the start I worked at obscuring them wherever I could - unfortunately with destructive consequences.

Exactly! As far as self-responsibility is concerned, I can just imagine someone going to their employer and saying: "Hey, I've caught the flu because I'm having trouble with my wife, and my heart is frozen up. It's my own fault, I'm going to make up for the lost working hours."

A person was constantly complaining about others. A wise man said to him: "If you really want peace, try to change yourself, not others. It is easier to protect your own feet with shoes than to walk barefoot and wish the whole world were covered with leather." (Teaching Stories)

Nobody would admit it, but one way or another it would almost always be the truth.

I don't know if my readers will be happy to hear that.

Nor will they want to hear that your specialists and experts are very susceptible to something else. Namely, their vanity. "Everything that can be invented has already been invented." This was said in 1899 by a leading engineer of the U.S. patent office. Would you like an example of the destructive power of this vanity?

Well, when I consider how Ignaz Semmelweis was treated in 1847 when he advised his fellow doctors to put on gloves when operating …

My example is even better: already half a century ago you could have developed a working, feasible and cheap technology for perfect energy management on earth exclusively with renewable energy sources. Instead, with my puppet Ronald Reagan, I steered the knowledge and manpower of thousands of experts and specialists towards prestigious and lucrative projects, such as in the oil industry. That has always been one of my easiest tasks. You can imagine what that would have meant for slowing down climate change alone.

Another example?

With pleasure. Given all your problems, what's the point of spending gazillions to plant a flag on the moon and bring home a few stones? And I think I don't have to explain what kind of motivation there is behind genetic engineering or the growth of security technology and weapons development. Nor do I have to explain what motivation drives you to ignore climate change. In many respects, you are still on the same level today as you were in the days of the brilliant ideas of river straightening and "consolidation of farms". From wooden spears to atomic bombs, that's what you call "progress".

Well, river straightening, we know today how idiotic that was. They thought, "We'll recover land - and in case of a flood, we'll redirect it further downstream."

Something else comes to mind: a few decades ago, doctors and experts recommended that kissing be restricted or even avoided altogether – because of the vast amount of bacteria and viruses that are "exchanged". Ten years later, a study proved that people who kiss a lot have a five year longer life expectancy on average than the "non-kissers".

As so often, love and common sense are wiser than any warning against bacteria.

And I remember that when the land was being consolidated, it was based on the conviction that the fields could be cultivated much more efficiently.

To do what? To make big farms even bigger, at the expense of quality, and to be able to supply McDonald's more cheaply thanks to soil and climate-destroying machinery? To remove fertile soil and deprive it of all living things?

You're right, we lost sight of that back then. Or deliberately ignored it.

Carry on, read a little more on the subject, preferably information from Greenpeace or PETA. Then you will get to know the interconnections better. However, you only really understood and made it public when the people who had come up with the idea of land consolidation had died or were only able to cause damage to their own gardens after retirement. Which they did: consequently private garden soil is five times more pesticide-ridden than agricultural topsoil.

Let's change the subject, please; otherwise my pessimism about the future will overwhelm me. Can we talk about your goals again? Where else have you been at work?

Well, as I said before: to transform you into creatures of habit and to rock you to sleep, that was my way and my task. Let's take a closer look: to transform any action into a habit and an automated routine by learning and practicing is indeed an important skill, for example when driving a car or operating a machine. However, in so many areas of life, forming a habit has a weakening effect, for example in nutrition, but particularly in your mind. In this way, a habit turns into a mental crutch or develops into an addiction, an obsession even.
How about a devil hack that tells you where the line is between a habit and an addiction? *Just stop doing it for at least seven days.* The degree of addiction will become apparent from the ensuing physical and mental withdrawal symptoms. The restlessness, the irritability, the fears, the headaches.

Sounds like a useful method. For example, when I think about what happens if I give up espressos for a few days ...

Look at a person's ageing process from this perspective, and you will realize how successful I have been at my work. Because, for most of you, ageing is "automatically" a gradual process of sinking into more and more habits, in the field of nutrition, clothing, exercise, ways of thinking, fears, right down to hair styles, etc. You even call this more or less colorful blend of habits the "unique character of a person" or even his "identity".

I tell you: if in a certain situation a person *cannot help* but think, feel or act in a fixed or rigid, predictable way, he's no longer a human being but a robot. And it doesn't matter at all if he can't help but be "good".

Your strongest sleeping pill is not some chemical sorcerer's concoction from the pharmacy but rather taking something "for granted" in your mind – be it a thing, a person, a future event, a "legally certified privilege", a monthly state pension. May I translate the sentence "I take that for granted!"?

Well, there's nothing stopping you.

"Now and in the future, the world has to meet my personal expectations!" My friend, only three things are self-evident: the casting off of your earthly garment, the right to learn, and Buddy´s love. May I offer you another translation? What is a "surprise"?

I'm already curious.

> *Freedom belongs to the essence of love. As soon as compulsion, control and conflicts arise, love dies. The rose, the tree and the land also let you be completely free. The tree will not make any effort to pull you into its shade if a sunstroke threatens. The lamp will not force its light on you if you stumble in the dark. (Anthony de Mello)*

Translated into reality it means: "unexpectedly disappointed expectation" or "unexpectedly fulfilled hope".

What you call "stroke of luck" is often no more than the expectation that something will go badly, and then it turns out well after all. Hooray! A stroke of luck!

Conversely, you call it "bad luck" when you expect that everything will go according to plan, but things turn out for the worse, and you moan about "bad luck". In this work of locking you into habits I had, by the way, as already indicated, the best helpers in your eating habits. **The devil hack here: recognize and understand without a doubt that your expectations and fears**

are your own decision. You can choose how you control your thoughts and emotions.

The majority would disagree! Okay, but now tell me: in what way can my eating habits, my favorite foods, help you succeed?

Your current normal diet, particularly in the cafeterias of businesses, factories and even hospitals, makes you incredibly tired and lethargic and thus colors a large part of your everyday life. You have absolutely no idea how much your eating habits have played into my hands! That was the ideal sphere for entrenching habits, both good and bad. The habit of considering meat or dairy, which have only been on your menu for a relatively short time, as "healthy food" – what a delusion! Only your short-term memory and aggressive public relations are responsible for this… and even your archaeologists to some extent.

But it is common knowledge that meat-centered nutrition is part of human heritage. Are the archaeologists wrong here?

You bet they are. They didn't take into account the fact that vegetable stews or cereal meals leave behind hardly any fossilized remains. They're almost completely composted, as you can perhaps understand. Bones are much more durable. The discovery of hunting weapons and animal bones made them overlook the fact that a diet lacking in animal protein leaves very little in the way of tangible remains. And there is something else they overlooked or did not classify correctly: if they were exploring remnants of primitive societies whose diet was meat-centered by necessity, their bones and teeth showed all the signs of the diseases of modern civilization: bone loss, arthritic joints, tooth decay, etc.

That makes sense. Recently I read that, for example, the Inuit of the Arctic Circle have very bad teeth.

They're forced to follow a meat- and fat-centered diet, that's the reason. It was always really dangerous for the success of my work when an influential person woke up and publicly renounced animal protein, sugar, white flour, etc.

So vegans are a thorn in your side? What makes them so special? Can they escape from you?

Absolutely! At least in the first weeks and months, after giving up the tiring “stuff-bloat-fill” diet, their sensitivity awakens and they get close to what was most dangerous for me: a clear awareness of their actual, objective situation, and to genuine self-love, leading to real progress of their souls. In other words, when they use the newly gained physical freshness and alertness for their own real benefit. When they focus their sharpened perception on what is *genuine and true*, to follow a path of development and self-realization, and to see through all the fake news. When that happened all I saw of them was a cloud of dust! But what a surprise - often it was all too easy to slow them down again.

Stuff-bloat-fill diet – a good description of what's put on our plates sometimes. In any case, not sustenance for life. I think I'll have to pay more attention to cooking healthy food. But how did you manage to "slow down" vegans? Are there special stumbling blocks in their path?

Stumbling blocks? No, no obstacles but rather lures and bait. Placing obstacles, that's something for novice devils. Barriers are easy to recognize, you can avoid them. No, temptations work much better. The targeted person can then maintain the illusion of being master of his own decisions. The ideal slave is under the illusion that he serves the tyrant of his own free will.
I've always done it this way: have you ever met an inveterate, diehard vegan? They can be insufferable, their pride in their achievements oozing out of every pore. They can often be so irritating that they put many people off following this valuable way of life. After all, who wants to become so narrow-minded? Great, fanatics like these were right up my street. Useful foot soldiers in our ranks.

Not suitable role models, so to speak ...

I fed their pride in being "special", which blocked the success of their convictions. Furthermore, the vegan movement has created a second barrier to the acceptance of their world view. They have overlooked the fact that for half of humanity the consumption of plant-based oils and fats is not healthy in the long run.

I've written about that!

That's right, as you know, the other half needs animal fat in the form of butter or clarified butter like Ghee. This gap in the vegan diet is large enough to put the brakes on its success for the time being.
A super devil hack at this point: ***if you have something good and genuine to convey, you simply have to exemplify its meaning and value. Don't get on anyone's nerves, don't try to convince anyone. Only then you will have long-term success.*** The art of persuasion? That's often equivalent to the art of brainwashing.

Hmm, sounds convincing, but some parents of adolescent rebels will not get away with just being a role model and setting good examples.

Oh right, your famous "adolescent rebellion". It will surprise you, but it is anything but an inevitable, "natural" developmental step, no matter what your clever parenting guides and experts drum into you. Such a rebellion develops because of the simple fact that many teenagers can rely on their intuitive faculties. They instinctively feel, "if I obey my parents, I will become just like them." And then they say to themselves, "Who wants that, after all?" If you would only let your kids find their own path in life and let go of them, and only intervene when there is real danger and hardship looming, there would be no rebellion.

"It seems so impractical to think of Buddy all the time," a visitor once told Yogananda. The answer was: "The world totally agrees with you – but is the world happy? Anyone who leaves Buddy, the epitome of bliss, is looking in vain for true happiness. True God seekers already live on Earth in the inner heaven of peace; but the others who forget it spend their days in the self-created underworld of uncertainty and disappointment. Thus, whoever makes friends with Buddy acts in a truly practical way." (Teaching Stories)

That strikes a chord with me! I was already rebelling at the age of six, but rather fruitlessly, without real intention or impact, just to get more attention and flexibility .
The three grownup children of close friends of ours never really needed to rebel. Today they are going completely different ways, independently of their parents´ life plan. Despite disagreements in the family, they nevertheless stick together like glue when it comes to the crunch. It's nice to see how they respect each other's differences.
But back to the topic of habit: isn´t any kind of learning comparable to acquiring a habit? What's wrong with turning new behavior into a useful habit that saves energy and brainpower?

From my point of view as the devil? All wrong if the habit is meaningful, fruitful and useful. Totally right, if it renders you immobile. Habits of thought often turn into mental inertia. Inertia solidifies into taboos of thinking and feeling. Your world then becomes very small, an island, a prison. You learn to despise and fear what is beyond the island. You learn to think in black and white, you rectify the normal until it turns into a ball and chain on your leg. You learn to fear what is flowing and alive.
You then turn what was once perhaps meaningful activity into meaningless "tradition" and into dependence. Traditions can be a wonderful thing, from parades, costumes, holidays, to demonstrations of ingenious craftsmanship in a particular part of the

world, the festival of ice sculptures, and so on. But I tell you, how I have loved traditions! Some of them are so massively destructive of what is right and necessary and yet there is always someone successfully defending them with the argument "we've always done it this way".

… I understand: if habits, traditions, customs, manners, rituals make me happy and optimistic, then they're okay. But if they only bring numbness, boredom, tired repetition without meaning, forget it, right?

Would you like some examples of the destructive form of tradition?

Celebrating Hitler's birthday?

That's one. But I rather thought of the farmer near your village who shouts out a cheerful "we´ve always done it this way!" in your direction when his tractor tears up the earth. I thought of your industrial agriculture which is, slowly but surely, turning the earth into a desert. When people started to impose these "modern" methods all over the world, the fertile soil measured on average more than two feet down. Today it's less than one foot. Not far from turning into desert, is it? In Europe, in large areas of Spain, it won't take long for grass, let alone tomatoes, to stop growing there. Do you know how many pounds of grain it takes to produce one pound of beef?

Two?

Sixteen. Truly, your habits, or better, your stubbornness has always been one of my closest allies. My friends, there is nothing, nothing at all, that you "have always done this way"!

Hmm, industrial agriculture has always defended itself with the claim that it has to feed a world population of almost ten billion people.

That is an absolute and deliberate lie on the part of "interested parties" - I'll tell you more about that later. Now - something to ponder: what is the difference between a hunter and the hunted?

You mean man and animal?

I mean hunter and hunted. Whether a hunter succeeds, or the prey escapes, depends on the predictability of behavior, in other words, on predictable routine. A hunter observes and remembers the routines of his prey until he succeeds. Someone being hunted will always escape if his movements are not predictable. The more routines and habits a living being has, the easier it becomes a victim. Example? The Emperor of Farfaraway becomes the hunted when he craves a small chocolate heart every Thursday morning. If he doesn't get it, he'll become so angry that he almost has a heart attack and can no longer think clearly. So who is the true emperor? Is it he? Or is it the one who brings him the chocolate heart? *That's why* one of my most successful strategies was to let you fall into habits. Every successful advertisement is based on the knowledge of the behavioral, thinking and feeling routines of its targets, victims, prey.

And recognizing and acting upon these patterns is the business model of social media …

Exactly. "Carry on as we always have" – that was music to my ears. Particularly in the area of the relationship between the sexes, this was important for my work because it helped to prevent true happiness between lovers.

Excuse me? You'll have to explain that in more detail!

People who truly love one another are almost immune to me – no matter if man and woman, woman and woman, man and man. But just look at the arrogance with which men all over the world present themselves as *by nature* "better", "more intelligent", "more industrious" than women! Even today! For the hidebound patriarchs on your planet, you and I have to come up with special devil hacks, because patriarchy is one of the most pernicious forces on this earth. Elderly white-tinted blockheads have succeeded in portraying the antagonisms in the world as an innate part of human nature, all that rivalry and willingness to use violence! I must confess, that was with my help, of course, but I'm a little scared when I look back and see that some of you were even better at it than me …

You're trying to convince me that the devil has a conscience?

My friend, I'm one of Buddy´s best friends and colleagues. I have a clear mission, but at the same time also a life of my own and my very own values. Otherwise I wouldn't be sitting here.

Here's my devil hack to dismantle the patriarchy in the long run: **you have to spread the word that all people in the world have the right to surround themselves exclusively with people who appreciate, respect and love them. Never suffer fools or negative people gladly – and be it your own mother or father.**

Remember? My friend Jesus said: **“No one who has left home or brothers or sisters or mother or father or children or fields for me and the gospel, will fail to receive a hundred times as much in this present age: homes, brothers, sisters, mothers, children and fields—along with persecutions—and in the**

age to come eternal life.” If you would all recognize, feel and enact this devil hack, this absolute human right, I predict that far fewer people in your senior citizens´ homes would be paid a visit than before. There would be far less traffic on Thanksgiving Day. And many men would be very lonely from one day to the next.

At fifteen I turned to learning,
at thirty I had solid ground.
At forty I had no doubts.
At fifty I knew the will of the heavens.
At sixty I was willing to listen to it.
At seventy I could follow the wishes of the heart,
without violating that which is right.
(Confucius)

In my case, you're preaching to the converted. For me, patriarchy has always entailed a gigantic waste of the skills that women naturally bring with them. Macho men only shoot themselves in the foot when they declare that women are "worth less" than men. These guys have placed themselves on a pedestal that would wobble all too quickly if they had to admit that they couldn't hold a candle to many women. And they resist the fact that women are no longer willing to be domestic slaves. Of course, some feminists overshoot the mark, but to me, thousands of years of oppression are justification enough even for a few exaggerations.

Over time, you men have simply repressed an irrefutable fact, namely that women, by nature, bring along special abilities. Compared to men, for example, they are compelled to have a much more practical mind!

Otherwise there would be no more babies to allow your souls to return to this place. "If men had to have babies, humanity would soon be extinct" – there's a grain of truth even in that stupid saying.
Men – often even powerful, dignified men holding high office – tend to make more emotional and unreasonable decisions than women in the same situation. The fairy tale that it is the other way around was invented by men – of course, encouraged by yours truly. You men are experts in wasting your women's abilities and talents, just as I intended.

Recently I read that the director of Harvard University justified the fact that there are fewer women than men in highly paid university professions by claiming that women are not willing to sacrifice eighty hours a week for their profession. What impudence! It's precisely the other way around: men are not willing to do what those women are doing who are supporting and backing the highly paid men with the eighty hours a week.
But not all is perfect in the world of women, is it? Margaret Thatcher, Theresa May, Imelda Marcos or the many women who fought feminism, even the right for women to vote!? Thatcher! Couldn't be more arrogant and heartless! And a very significant symptom: many women stab their best friend in the back when she breaks out of a situation of exploitation.

As anywhere else, "exceptions prove the rule", my friend. Lady Thatcher was very eager to learn the tricks of my business, indeed. And of course also Eva Braun, Grace Mugabe, Mirjana Milosevic, Imelda Marcos, Margot Honecker … Many others behind the scenes have goaded quite a few male dictators to his alleged “greatness”.

For what reason?

Well, their being women made it easier for them to recognize that the real power brokers on this planet always pull strings in the background, unrecognized. Their ego was not in the way. The really powerful ones in the world are successful because they are oriented towards results, not medals, decorations, ovations. No chance of bribing them. A few of your conspiracy theories are anything but theory.
Secondly, these women wanted to fill the emptiness in their souls by balancing their own weakness with the supposed strength of the one they lifted up. This is, of course, only an illusion. The same illusion that makes the supporter of a soccer team happy when “his” team wins. I always have to laugh when the ‘Munchhausens’ who write your history books pin the epithet “The Great” on some puer aeternas that just doesn't want to grow up. But that tendency also played into my hands.

“Baron Munchhausen”? The famous liar? But not all of them, right? There are some great history books that just cannot be

misconstrued, let alone suborned to shore up an artificial ideology, thereby falsifying history.

Being able to present history in an exciting and interesting way says nothing about the truth of what is written. To perceive, describe and write down what actually happens, that's a very great and very rare art form. Do you know the story of the circus elephant?

Perhaps ...

It goes like this:
Once upon a time, long, long ago, there was a small town whose inhabitants had never seen an elephant before. When one day a circus set up its tents there, advertising an elephant, a few brave ones set out one by one at night to explore the eerie creature in the darkness of the animal cage.
A philosopher stroked the elephant's trunk, returned home and lectured his wife about the snake-like nature of the strange animal.
A doctor was able to grasp a leg and then told his astonished children about the creature´s rough surface, its gigantic weight and the fact that the elephant was hardly distinguishable from the columns at the entrance to their town hall.
A poet stroked an ear of the animal several times and then wrote a poem at home about the elephant

and its close relatives, the bats, which were however much smaller.
Finally, a brave little girl sneaked into the tent and lit a candle first.
So who do you want to entrust with the writing of history, with what result?

I already know the story, but you made up the ending!

Right, you got me there! But even the girl will write her own story about the elephant, light or no light. But we were talking about patriarchy. Usually it is men like Trump or my disciples in the Ku Klux Klan or the religious fanatics who have to compensate for despair, weakness and hatred of their parents by oppressing others – especially women. My work has always been to inspire such men to confuse mental and physical acts of violence with invincible strength and willpower. They bounced like puppets who believed it was they themselves pulling the strings. Ingenious! Boy, sometimes I just couldn't stop patting myself on the back. By the way, you haven't even begun to understand the immense damage that a "democratically" elected man like Trump has caused in the long run.

Well, I have at least an inkling! Almost the whole world has aligned itself with the USA as leading power, from the music to the dream of rising from rags to riches, which is supposed to be much easier here. That's why the shock of being presented with such a childish tyrant is so great everywhere. The real catastrophe is the lowering of the moral baseline for followers of such role models. All over the world, cold misanthropic populists are once again gaining ground because they have pulled previously hidden prejudices, aversion to "others" and general feelings of hatred to the surface and made them socially acceptable. Yet again women are even being told that they should put up with their 'naturally subordinate' positions.

That the woman should be "subservient" to the man – whoever came up with claiming this was Buddy´s idea deserves the Golden OUW even today! To treat people of whatever origin and skin color like property and slaves is exactly the same as if you treated and exploited your twin brother like an animal just because he was born two minutes after you.

Seems that we humans still have a lot of work ahead of us. Now what is the "Golden OUW"?

The "OUW"? That's the "Oscar of the Underworld", which we used to award whenever we were feeling bored in the office. An "underworld" doesn't exist, of course, but we found your beliefs and dogmas here so funny that the label stuck.

Well, a few candidates for the honorary award spring to mind, among them one of my teachers, whose greatest pleasure was to humiliate students in malicious ways. At the age of forty-five, he was still living with his mother. At that time, one of my fellow students actually said: "The devil has sent us that man."

I asked for strength
and Buddy gave me trouble that strengthens me.
I asked for wisdom and Buddy
gave me problems to solve.
I asked for prosperity
and Buddy gave me brains and muscles to work.
I asked for courage
and Buddy gave me dangers to cope with.
I asked for love
and Buddy gave me troubled people I can help.
I asked for grace and favor
and Buddy gave me opportunities.
I received nothing of what I asked for,
and yet I received everything. Buddy bless you.
(Renée Thompson)

Oops, I did, I remember. Sorry, but I never spared anybody. That was just my job, as you might have come to realize by now. Among prospective "OUW" candidates are all those who judge a person by skin color, religion and sexual preferences. Some of you were even one step ahead of me here. The most recent "OUW" was awarded to a bishop who not only succeeded in covering up sexual exploitation in the Catholic Church, but was also one of the perpetrators himself.

Indeed a hot topic, but thank god, some of them are finally being taken down.

You shouldn't be thankful to Buddy, you have to thank yourselves, especially some brave women among you.

Ah, right, free will … Then you're also responsible for the fact that children of parents of different skin color and religion are often treated as outsiders, aren't you? I was lucky to grow up without major prejudices, and so I could see that such children usually develop into special and often interesting and beautiful people. In any case, I found that the denigration of such people as "half-castes" originates in envy and, of course, also in fear, because they are living proof that it's possible to cross barriers without forfeiting any happiness in life – in fact, the opposite.

You're right - I'm getting to like you more and more. I've worked hard to conceal that fact from you. And above all, I have encouraged the opposite idea, namely that such people remain alienated from their parents' environment – dissidents, bastards even. I worked hard to turn neutral descriptive terms like bastard, crossbreed, half-breed and so on into insults.

But I worked even harder at disguising the special characteristics of these people – from their usually attractive appearance all the way to their special ability to build bridges between worlds. Because the children of parents of different origins were and are particularly suited to promoting understanding between antagonistic groups, especially between black and white, red and white, black and Latino, Jews and Christians, Muslims and Christians, Hindus and Muslims, etc. The parents of such people are mostly fully aware of the hostility from their environment, yet they still form their relationship. This usually testifies to a deep, genuine love between them. That, in turn, is the best basis for raising well-behaved children who, in addition, learn almost automatically to cope with the hostility of their environment without suffering too much physical or emotional harm. Such parents and their children almost always have a stimulating and enriching effect on their environment, in the best sense, if that environment is open and curious.

I wasn't aware of these interconnections until now, but now that I come to think about it, you're right. Back in my schooldays, I was more interested in companions who were somehow "different". I always wanted to find out what was special about them. By the way - the cock-and-bull story that it's a sign of unmanliness and weakness when men show feelings – you know, "real men don't cry" – this myth, you're responsible for that, too, aren't you? You must be, because this bullshit is directly and indirectly responsible for so much suffering in the world.

Right, but here I have only sown a few seeds for which you were the fertile soil: fathers today who are still proud of sons who act like insensitive class tyrants and mini machos instead of calmly making them aware of the consequences of their actions. Or mothers who punish their daughters more severely than their sons for the same misdemeanors. Then you recognize who is using his free will to what end. The devil hack here: meditate on this truth:

Violence is real weakness.
Love, harmony and togetherness are real strength.

Well, I'll certainly take that to heart!

That's praiseworthy, but a word of caution: this is something deeply rooted in you men. You are so male-dominated and patriarchal in all your institutions that, for example, accused rapists here in the USA are acquitted in forty-eight out of fifty cases. That speaks volumes and can be observed all over the world.
One of my masterpieces was not only that people who happen to be lighter skinned grow up with the

conviction that this lighter "coating" will turn them into something "better", or even worse: more intelligent than those people whose skin color tends more towards black, red or yellow. Throughout history, I also have succeeded in instilling in you men the conviction that someone who is capable of using more violence than an other – by physical force or by the use of weapons – is endowed with an inbuilt permission to behave inhumanely and to be celebrated as "The Great". As if the lust for murder, lust for power and violence were to transform a human being into something "higher" than what he really is and which certainly would not deserve a prominent place in history books. After all, you are resourceful. Whites, for example, treat Blacks like dirt from the very beginning and then take worse school grades as "proof" of Whites' supremacy. Or tie an iron ball to a Black's leg and look at him with contempt because he runs more slowly than you.

A famous sculptor was working on a marble lion. Full of admiration, a visitor asked him about the secret of his craft and art. The master answered: "That's not so difficult at all. I simply chisel away everything that does not look like a lion." (From Arabia)

In my experience, you're right. And I recall history class. From battle to battle … Very quickly, by the way: I've always wondered whether there is actually a difference between right-wing and left-wing extremist violence.

No. Only in name and frequency. Also to some extent as far as the spiritual roots of the ideologies are concerned. Right-wing extremists are almost always on an unconscious vendetta against their fathers and long for the strong father figure who says "you're okay, you're one of us, a good comrade". Left-wing extremists are often taking revenge on their cold families and long for a feeling of security and comfort in the group against the evil world. They miss a reliable mom. Here is the reason why the left is less hierarchically organized in your political spectrum than the right. Leftists are better at partisan fighting. At the most extreme ends, both take the easy way out, without common sense, empathy and heart. Those were good students in my courses.

The labelers in all kinds of media and news organizations will not like to hear this at all …

You must not conceive of left and right as being on a straight line but rather on a circle where the "center" is opposite to the extremes "left/right". Left-wing extremist and right-wing extremist, these are twin brothers connected by the rejection of self-responsibility, by spiritually inert black-and-white thinking, by the longing for the "we feeling" and unconditionality. They are considered "political" only to cover up that fact. Real politicians are true servants of your people.

I'll have to think about that. In any case, politics and the media will not give up their labelling habits so quickly…
Oh, speaking of labels: I'd like to know how you earned your infamous reputation. You know: Prince of Hell, and all that. Those extremely negative epithets like "devilish, diabolical". The stories and paintings depicting your alleged work are mostly repulsive and terrifying.
Oh, and does hell even exist as it has always been described to us in highly lurid tones? Just recently, the new "Buddy Deputy on Earth" in the Vatican… with just one stroke of a pen he declared that Purgatory does not exist after all – fooled ya! We may have frightened the flocks of sheep for thousands of years, but we're sorry – it's your own fault for falling for that nonsense.

Ingenious, right? All my own idea, the invention of "Purgatory". But to return to your first question: to invent me as the boss of an inhospitable place, preferably underground, in the midst of fiery streams of lava, surrounded by roasting human beings, rejected by Heaven, sizzling over a giant barbecue as punishment, that was one of my cleverest moves to throw you into physical, mental and spiritual dependence. Fear in any form has always been one of my most efficient weapons.

Fear, for example, of learning something new, because then it reveals your previous ignorance, or that the old was somehow not "right".

Fear of showing supposed weaknesses, because then you might get ridiculed.

Fear of criticism, fear of going to "hell", because you have "sinned".

That's a keyword: "sin". Countless generations were scared into submission by dangling it over their heads.

Not just by me. The invention of sin, well, I hardly had to lift a finger because peddlers of religion the world over have done such a great job. They simply turn anything into "sin" that would saw away at their unholy throne.

Almost everything that makes you free and independent is turned into sin. That every child comes into the world afflicted with "original sin", this low point of all abominable lies, would not have occurred even to me, that's how far away from the truth this is. You do not bring along original sin but an excess of joy of life and enthusiasm.

So there's no such thing as original sin? Well, I've never believed in it, but I'd be quite gob smacked to hear you confirm that ... it would make me happy and confirm my own conviction.

Before I reply to that, I would like to point out a connection, a small final word on the subject of "patriarchy". Because a certain circumstance is too important not to deserve at least a mention.

I'm listening.

Good. Every human being that exploits another human being, who treats them as "less worthy", who looks down upon other human beings, automatically loses his self-respect. Consciously or unconsciously. Regardless of whether man or woman.

How can that be? Look at all those tyrants and oppressors! Look at the cultures where domestic violence is the norm. The majority of women out there experience domestic violence, and these men do not really act as if they have any particular doubt about themselves and their behavior! The examples of men feeling completely self-righteous when they act like primitive macho men are endless.

Ingenious, isn't it? In this respect, my work was extremely successful - unfortunately, I must say today. But you are utterly wrong. Those tyrants and exploiters may be completely unscrupulous in carrying out their work, but still, they've paid a price for it because they have put their innate love for humanity, the depths of their soul, to sleep. They no longer have any self-respect. In your experience, how does a person deal with this?

Hmmm, there are different options. Many fall into a deep depression. But I think most of them become even more violent over time to silence their inner voice. Some commit suicide by degrees, by developing a chronic sickness. Some do manage to become aware of their situation and find their way back to being human. From Saul to Paul. Many years ago I had a customer in my taxi who treated me like a lowly servant. At the end of the ride, I turned around and asked him why he was so afraid of life. He started crying and told me half of his life story.

I see you understand. So let's turn to your previous question, whether or not there is original sin. Sin, as you use the term in everyday life, generally does not exist, and certainly not in the form of your perverse fantasy of a "mortal sin".

So then there's also no punishment for sins.

No, there's not. There are consequences. As you sow, so you reap. What goes around, comes around. You've just succeeded in hiding the fact that the harvesting and the "coming around" sometimes take a long time. Only a few of you succeed in overcoming the laws of nature.

Okay, maybe we should do away with the word "sin". But after all, there are things that can be botched up or made a mess of. Sometimes a really big mess …

You have been told
that life is darkness,
and in your weariness
you echo what was said
by the weary.
And I say that life is indeed darkness, save when there is urge, and all urge is blind, save when there is knowledge,
and all knowledge is vain, save when there is work,
and all work is empty, save when there is love;
and when you work in love, you bind yourself to yourself,
to one another, and to Buddy.
(Khalil Gibran)

Of course. This is what actually happens: mistakes, misapprehensions and diversions. Whether any act or thing is indeed a mistake is directly dependent upon the goal you want to achieve, the direction you're taking. As George Harrison sang: "If you don't know where you're going, any road will get you there."

If you start from New York and want to get to San Francisco by the fastest route, you've made a mistake if, after a few days, you pass the sign "Arctic Circle" and you wonder whether you have packed the wrong clothes in your suitcase. But it was no sin!
Mistakes are what you make. The only disadvantage is that, with every repetition of the same mistake, you increase the probability of making that mistake again and again. Then you have turned it into a habit or an addiction. But even then you can turn around and start all over again. Do you know the actual meaning of the word "repentance"?

For most people it probably means having a bad conscience.

However, that does not bring with it any guarantee of improvement. My friend on the other side, Paramahansa Yogananda, he grasped it when he said: "Don't constantly think about all the things you did wrong in the past. Focused attention evokes habits and memories and gives them strength. Therefore, you should not focus your attention on the bad deeds. Banish them from your mind and ensure that you do not repeat such actions. True repentance does not mean what you have been told and had crammed down your throat. It means end of the error and a new beginning, not self-accusation and guilty conscience."

So instead of sin one could use the term dead end, or even detour …

You are getting closer. How about a handy example concerning your strange conception of "sin"?

Gladly. It probably has something to do with sex.

The candidate has ten out of ten points. Physical love, this ingenious gift from Mama Buddy, you have – unfortunately under my guidance – turned it into something "dirty", like nasty graffiti in subway underpasses. Your religious pushers then instructed you that, on the blessed day of the wedding, it will miraculously transform into something heavenly, which must be given to your spouse, daintily wrapped in ribbon bows. And as if that's not enough, it's combined with a strengthening of the patriarchy, because the bride has to "give it" whereas the husband "takes it". All this under the jurisdiction of the religious pushers, because sex is only permitted if there is a firm intention to beget as many children as possible. And also if it's not too much fun.

Ouch, you are describing Western Christian sex life in all its normality.

You have even created laws, under threat of severe punishment, forbidding teenagers to approach physical love and tenderness in small steps and with caution. Many of your laws are nothing but fears frozen in time, that are supposed to never melt in the warmth of love, courage and insight. At the same time you have, until today, not prevented the same initially cheerful and curious teenagers from watching brutal and disgusting pornography on their cell phones and children's room TVs. So what do they learn until they come of age?

Well, the opposite of being relaxed, happy and natural. But I've also noticed that porn and violent films are often so popular among young people because they can use them to distance themselves from strict parents, teachers and priests. Within the group or by themselves, they free themselves from the misconceptions of the adult world.

Correctly observed. And then they replace them with their own misconceptions. Think about pornography: one minute repulsive, a minute later a gift from Buddy. That can´t work, right? With thinking like that, you have turned gold into dirt, almost in the truest sense of the word. And into a stream of money flowing into the coffers of your psychotherapists, who almost never help you regain the joy and ease of a fulfilled sexuality. Why do they not succeed?

Because … no one can give what he does not possess himself?

You've hit the nail on the head!

Mamma mia, I've met many therapists in my life, fortunately never as a client. I've almost always asked myself: "Do I want to become like this person?" I once asked one of them: "In your work you try to become your client's best friend. If you succeed, how does it feel to have to break up with your new best friend again and again?" Instead of an answer, he started crying, and I had to try to comfort him.

Oh yes, the difference between theory and practice.
Touching skin itself is as vital and essential as the air that we breathe, particularly for babies and small children! You "adults" have turned it into something that has to be handled with the greatest caution, like working with explosives. Well, that's understandable when touch is abused for the purpose of humiliation. But there can be no healthy and loving child development without tenderness and touch.
Write it down: Without touch, you will raise obedient, cold-hearted soldiers but not human beings capable of love and harmonious relationships. Even later in life, touching, hugging, and caressing are as vital as air and water, even in old age. Truly, in some things you are better than me.

Hang on a sec, we´ll have to talk about that in more detail.

With pleasure, it's an important topic. But first let's get back to your previous question. Your peddlers of religion have let themselves be seduced by me to create the fantasy of a "hell". But hell doesn't exist.

It doesn´t exist. I see.

No, it does not exist in the way you imagine it – except in your heads. Peddlers of religion have dabbled in this fata morgana to rule with carrot and stick, and to keep people in a state of mental and physical dependence. Behind that is pure lust for power. Hell is something self-made, which comes into being in your mind, and is kept alive by a poisonous mixture of fear, stubborn conviction, greedy expectation, crude prejudice and intellectual taboos. You are creating hell in your own lifetime.

So there's no hell after death, either? That would be a comfort …

Nope. No hell is waiting for you, not for anyone.

Not for anyone? That´s a little hard to believe! What is waiting then for Hitler, Pol Pot and all the others? And for the terrorists who blow themselves up, along with many innocent people? When it comes to that, I'd like to have the certainty that they will get what they deserve!

When I was a child,
my mother taught me the traditions of our people. She told me about the sun and the sky, the moon and stars, the clouds and the winds.
She also taught me to kneel down and ask the Great Spirit for strength, health, wisdom and protection.
At no time were our prayers directed against others.
(Geronimo, chief of the Chiricahua Apaches)

Justified question, but not easy to answer if you expect it to be a consolation to your sense of justice. Perhaps the following truthful answer will comfort you:
In the course of the many hundreds of thousands of years of a soul's journey, it experiences all justice, all love, all experiences, all feelings, all knowledge, all meaning that the universe and Buddy are capable of. Absolute justice for every human being, it exists.
What you do to others, you'll experience yourself. Perhaps not in this lifetime, but in another.
The good things you do will always return to you. Perhaps not in this lifetime but in another.

But then Hitler, Stalin and so on – they'll have to endure a lot, won't they?

Correct, but not in the way you assume. You shouldn't rack your brains about it. May it cheer you up – absolute justice exists. There is one aspect that all you people shouldn't lose sight of: that without their helpers, these tyrants would amount to almost nothing. For the most part, they were puppets dancing to others' tunes.

Well, if I leave it at that, I am sure there are some who would regard that as a justification for these mass murderers.

It's exactly the other way round, my friend: to put all the blame on these mass murderers kicks the door wide open for all their cohorts and minions to shed their own responsibility. You certainly know the motto of the puppets? "I was only obeying orders."

Everyone who is looking for a way to get rid of all humaneness and self-responsibility knows these words.

Right. But let's get back briefly to the subject of "hell". As far as the moment of your soul's return to its home is concerned, perhaps for the thousandth time, you yourself are in charge each time. You yourself are responsible, if you, with your mental powers, drag a homemade hell over there along with you and keep it alive for a time. With some souls, it can take centuries of earth time until they see the light that would have been waiting for them from the very beginning. It is your personal decision how long you wait until you finally return home, to the place where the soul belongs. Even a "Last Judgment", as you were taught, does not exist.

My goodness, that's an essential instrument of spiritual torture in almost all religions!

No "Last Judgment", my friend. This idea of some kind of criminal court or tribunal was also one of my inventions, in combination with what I´ve suggested to you about hell. Again, simple carrot and stick tactics. Well, maybe a little too much stick here, sorry. What is waiting for you instead is a friendly discussion about the lifetime just finished, with the question as to whether you have reached all your goals. Yes? Fine! No? Well, next time then …

Hmmm, I can't imagine that some of these debriefings proceed in such a pleasant way.

Well yes, they do. Because, first of all, it sometimes takes a long time for the soul to overcome her feelings of guilt to finally come to this conversation. And secondly, the queasy feeling that some will, rightly or wrongly, bring to the discussion is solely their own self-made baggage. Your soul-guides wish you well at all times, and they bring along endless patience.

Okay, the stick was hell and judgment day, but they don't exist; instead, friendly advice. So far so good. But what about the carrot "paradise"? Doesn't it exist either? So much wasted anticipation among the good and pious …

Legitimate question. If you have followed the ways of the world attentively, you'll find, on the one hand, that the hope or even promise of a paradise has been abused by very bad people. Extreme example: "Blow yourself up, along with some infidels, and you will enter paradise." This form of paradise does not exist. Such deluded people are in for quite a surprise afterwards.

Well, I'm really glad to hear that!

Paradise, on the other hand, is in a certain sense your true home, but not only "over there", after you have cast off your temporary garment called the "body", but already here, in this dimension. Because "over there" is not a physical place, as you envision it. It is as "here" as the air that surrounds you. But you cannot grasp and experience it directly, just as a blind person can´t experience the rainbow. Paradise is simultaneously here as it is there, simultaneously your home as it is further away than the most distant planet. It is all a question of willingness and ability…

Could you get any more enigmatic?

Well, how should I put it? Roughly speaking, imagine you are surrounded by radio and TV stations, but you don't own a radio or television set, and you have never before seen such devices and have no idea what they are. So what chance would I have to correctly describe to you what "radio" and "television" mean? Most likely you would declare me whacko because "images and sounds from faraway countries that whiz through the air," are mumbo-jumbo. You see, here on earth you are immersed in another reality to which you simply lack the "radio" for the moment. But exactly THAT is the challenge! Build yourself this radio! Tune in to other wavelengths! This is why meditation was invented. Meditation is building an antenna!

Well, that resonates with the one or two experiences I've already had while meditating.

Yes, and what awaits you after death is first and foremost your own creation; everybody creates his or her own heaven or hell with their mind. If you allow yourself after a shorter or longer period of time to perceive the reality behind your subjective creations, then there will be a reunion with your best friends, the members of your true circle of friends; your gang, who have stuck together through thick and thin for thousands of years. If you wish, there will be a happy and joyful reunion party. And only then do you sit down with your friends and guides for a revision of your previous round – what went well and what could have been better, and maybe will be next time. In the process, however, you always have the last word. You decide on the when and the how. And even if at all. To sum up: Heaven is the real home for every woman and man.

Stop, stop! Most readers are probably asking themselves now: how can all this be my personal decision and an expression of my free will? The existence of Heaven and Hell and the Last judgment is forced down our throats as ultimate truth with our mother's milk, with thousands of sermons in church, by our parents, at school…!

Correctly worded. "Forced down your throats" is the right term for that. But who gives permission for such force-feeding? Who says "yes" to these ruthless inhumane teachings? Who allows such brainwashing to enter your mind so that truth is no longer admitted? I´ve always relied on you to accept my fake news passively and gullibly, but who stands at the gate of your mind, lets the garbage in and even pays for it?

Allow your mind to observe the truth directly. You will realize that, in every such case of brainwashing, there is also some form of exchange involved. It yields profit to believe that crap – and above all, in showing publicly that you believe it.
Because then you are "One of the Guys"! You belong! First to family and friends, then to cliques, then to group and party, then to whatever else! Then you just have to repeat the appropriate beliefs and convictions often enough, and lo and behold! You accept for true and real what in reality is only hot air, even if it has been polluting the air for thousands of years.

Most people want to change the world, but not themselves. The others have to change. Those up there, they mumble down below. Those below, cry those above. The men, say the women. The women, say the men.
We begin to threaten and to exert pressure. It is so hard for us to understand that nobody has the right to force others to change. Only conviction, friendship, good example and insight can bring others to change. Man is the only being that is capable of changing himself consciously. If people do not change, nothing changes. Change the world? I start again and again – with myself. (Phil Bosmans)

But who can defend himself successfully against this brainwashing; after all, it starts on the first day of life. That's what's called "education"! And anyway, what role does free will play in a baby's baptism? Or in a circumcision? The strength and insight to step out of the prison of dogma, or to overcome mental taboos, they all come much later in life, if at all. And the basic needs of belonging, of security and being appreciated and understood, they are all the more essential the younger one is! At least subjectively this is a question of survival!

What do you think, has a baby ever put on a friendly smile when his foreskin has been snipped off? It is your conviction that worked most effectively into my hands and made my work immensely easier. After all, you undermine the gift of free will and the ability to reach insights and arrive at free decisions even without my help from the very first day of life.

Instead of promoting these abilities, letting them develop and mature, all influencers work hand in hand – schools, psychologists, media, pushers of religion, lawyers – to crush in your children the natural spirit of independence, individuality, freedom of the will, until it disappears under mountains of beliefs and fears. Even a newborn baby has willpower, the power of discrimination and human dignity. It is anything but a blank sheet of paper just waiting to be scribbled all over by you, and to be shown the right way. It is anything but a freely pliable mass that many of your educators and psychologists declare it to be. Every baby brings more knowledge of human nature into the world than most of your so-called adults have.

The correct and ideal devil hack that can wipe out decades of brainwashing and preparation for victimhood, looks like this:

Want what you do.

Decide on a path.

Take responsibility.

Stand up for all consequences.

This devil hack applies to young and old, at any age!

Legions of psychologists will vehemently oppose this, because their premises and many of their therapies subtly take away the client's self-responsibility and blame childhood, trauma, circumstances, motives, etc. Of course it works really well, in that it extends therapy time indefinitely.

Right, to steer the issue of self-responsibility into obscure channels has been one of my main goals. Unfortunately very successfully, and you can read every day in the newspapers just how destructive it is. Some of the experts under my spell even tried to convince you that there is no such thing as free will.

A large part of my work was to close your eyes to the great treasure that your children bring into the world as a gift for you. After all, adults can learn much more from children than vice versa. Your children come into the world, completely and utterly perfect, inhabited by an indestructible soul, almost always with goodwill, natural kindness, a clear feeling for everything good, true and beautiful. With a vivid memory of the time before birth, of their true home. With a precise feeling for the meaning and purpose of their being here. They would know exactly what to do, look forward to it and want to embrace the world. Most of them keep this heavenly state of wakefulness for some months, sometimes even a few years. For many, however, that heavenly state is clouded over a few days after birth.

But that doesn't apply to all of them!

Yes, it does. Of course, some souls have burdened themselves with particularly difficult tasks before their return; they often dive very quickly into various swamps of earthly existence to get them done. These are then often "difficult" children who, despite all parental love, go astray.

It's getting a little hot in my head again ...

Keep cool, we´re getting there. Let's move on: to ensure that access to freedom, self-determination and free will is locked up as quickly and as long-term as possible, many centuries ago I put the concept of "being possessed" into people's minds. You just loved the idea! Anyone who did not want to obediently adapt to the prevailing habits of thought was quickly declared "possessed". Peddlers of religion and tyrants were especially keen on making use of this pseudo-reality, and declared as "possessed" anyone who didn't want to swallow the daily quantum of indoctrination and slavery, like the compliant sheep they were supposed to be. As icing on the cake, you invented "exorcism". Most of its survivors were sufficiently scared to get back in line as quickly as possible. And then what? Who was most often considered to be "possessed" and "bewitched" and seduced by demons?

Well, women for the most part ...

Correct! One more question: why do you think there were a thousand times more "witches" than male "sorcerers" and "wizards"?

Hell, now that you ask me ... you're right. Was it a particularly perfidious form of sexism?

Right again. The background? Throughout all times, women had better access to special aspects of knowledge – knowledge of herbs and healing secrets, of telepathy and other abilities that were blunted in men faster than in women.

Buddy is eternal bliss. His essence is love, wisdom and joy. He reveals himself as he pleases. He appears before his saints in the form that is most dear to them: the Christian beholds Christ, the Hindu sees Krishna or the Divine Mother, etc. Whoever worships something super-personal in Buddy perceives him as an infinite light or the Holy Spirit.

There are people who describe their Creator as a dictatorial and bossy being who befuddles man with ignorance and punishes him with fire, and who judges man's actions with heartless accuracy.

By doing so, they distort the true image of Buddy – that of the compassionate Heavenly Being – and paint a false image of him – that of a severe, ruthless and vengeful tyrant. However, anyone who is in contact with Buddy knows how foolish it is to imagine him as anything other than a compassionate being who holds infinite love and goodness within himself.

The highest experience that can be given to a human being is that bliss that fully embraces all other expressions of Buddy – love, wisdom, immortality. Try to get in touch with Buddy. It is possible to know Buddy as well as you know your dearest friend. That is the truth.

(Yogananda)

Why? Because these things can only be accessed through intuition, meditation and emotional depth – in other words, through direct perception! And these abilities were and still are lacking in the scripts for boys and men.

Rather the opposite, right?

Yes. This gap in male experience has led men to develop deep-seated fears of women over the millennia of patriarchy and, at the same time, a strong interest in suppressing them so as not to face their own fears. Because "fear is something only for the weak". Men had to suppress everything that reminded them of their own weaknesses.
Wise, vivacious women who were confident in their sexuality were therefore often branded as "possessed by demons" and attacked in various ways. Of course not only by fearful men but also out of cowardice by suppressed and indoctrinated women who feared for their own lives. The phenomenon is still highly visible today, when a woman fearlessly frees herself from a tormentor at home or in the workplace, and then her "best friends" shun her – just because they themselves do not dare take this step into freedom.

With my help, you have thoroughly repressed the fact that, as a rule, one fanatically fights only what one perceives in oneself and rejects out of fear.

The pieces of the puzzle are coming together; I understand. And I hope that many readers will see the light as well. So, do you perhaps still have a devil hack up your sleeve on how to pull the rug from under the patriarchy in the long run?

Of course, but you already know that one.

I think we have to start with small boys and treat them with the same love and tenderness that we usually reserve for girls. We have to set an example and show them that they are allowed to cry, to have weaknesses, to develop respect for other people. We must let them feel and experience unconditional love. In my experience, all cold patriarchs lacking empathy grew up without love and trust and genuine family ties. Change has to begin at exactly this point.

Right. You simply have to treat boys like human beings and not like objects of investment or continuations of yourselves.

Well then. On the subject of religions: so what's all this game about heaven and hell, nirvana and the underworld, this giant bouquet of religions, sects and beliefs? Why does this subject have such an enormous impact in everyday life, nearly everywhere in the world? If you look closely, there is no democracy, no secular government that is not afraid of the authorities of the great religions, and which would not give them permission to dictate to them what is right and what is wrong. Many so-called secular laws are merely reflections of artificial religious dogma. The USA has thousands of miles of beautiful beaches, but hardly anyone is permitted to happily go for a swim in their birthday suit, and even babies are forced into bikinis there. Mothers cover their children's eyes when a couple kiss on TV, and just recently a young German tourist couple were dragged to court in the USA because their three-year-old son was playing naked in a sandbox behind their own house.

All right, let's stay on the topic. A short lecture for beginners: the word "religion" originates from the Latin word *religare* which basically means "to reconnect" or "to connect back". Thus religion is the art of reconnecting something separated with a whole that would be its natural state. And what was it that was separated? And from what? *Well, you from Buddy! Which means, you from yourself!*

More detail here please! Otherwise I fear many readers will abandon us at this point. People are much less willing to question religious ideas and concepts than how they educate their kids.

Good. Since the beginning of time, True Religion has been a very diverse and highly individual method to remind the soul of its actual home, and to describe and facilitate the way back there. That way man can turn towards the path for which he was born this time around. That is the purpose of life for every human. The key is, at the end of the path there is always the realization that one was never really separated from home. It was all an illusion, a game!

And your task was to cloud this memory? You were supposed to block the ways back home, or seduce us into detours?

Exactly. I am to distract you from the true meaning of life. That was the devil's work from the beginning.

Oh, I would be interested to know how you describe the meaning of life …

The meaning of life is to love – yourself and others – and be loved,
never to stop being curious,
to learn and make beautiful what you come in contact with,
and be joyful in doing all that.
Until you have found the unity behind diversity again.

That rings true ...

You have written umpteen books to complicate or hide these simple truths. Your priests, imams, pastors, philosophers, monks, shamans, so many of them have been literally smashing each other´s heads in, in order to distort this truth so that their fear of life, their pride and lust for power find justification.

My goodness, that feels absolutely right. When I think about all that I've read without having gotten any wiser …

But you shouldn't complain because there are many correct guides and signs, even today. You yourself have received many valid hints concerning the "way back home", but often the information dripped off of your soul, like water off a duck's back. True religion does not hide, it is visible. In fact, it is much more visible than a hundred years ago. You can even google it, though it is not easily recognizable under all the Internet noise.

How's that possible? What are the search terms? How would I recognize them?

You are asking too much. You see, I am forbidden to actively carry people into the darkness. I'm only allowed to seduce them to go there of their own accord. Conversely I am also prevented from paving the way to the light for you. Buddy´s guide markers and signposts stand upright at all times, but nobody is carried across the finish line. That would turn the meaning of life into hot air without substance. Besides, that would be asking too much of the devil, wouldn't it? But I can help you to recognize True Religion when you encounter it, whether on the Internet, in books or elsewhere. Agreed?

That would be very helpful, not just for me …

Rely on Buddy when it comes to solving all your problems. Don't let paralysis spread over your courage and wits when, out of nowhere, an avalanche of big troubles tries to bury you. Keep your intuitive, healthy common sense and trust in Buddy and try to seize any chance for a solution, no matter how small – and you will find it!
Everything will ultimately work out for the best, because Buddy has hidden his goodness beneath the surface of the contradictory experiences of mortal existence. (Yogananda)

So: True Religion is a wake-up agent, it lets you wake up to what is.
It allows you to look not only behind some scenes and stage props but behind all scenes.
It's the absolute opposite of "Opium of the People". When coining this term, Karl Marx was referring to the

sedating drug sold by your religion peddlers. They fear nothing more than your awakening to the essence of True Religion.

True Religion leads to true faith, which is the faith Jesus meant, when he said that it moves mountains. An utterly wonderful, happy adventure – experienced, lived and taught by people who are true friends of all people, regardless of skin color, status, origin, orientation or preferences in their love lives.

True Religion is very quiet, it doesn't push or urge, doesn't do missionary work, does not persuade or seduce. It speaks quietly about itself and rejoices in every reply. It is completely certain of itself because it is genuine, natural and beautiful, and it is directed toward the genuine, natural and beautiful in man.

It is true and thus does not need, even for a second, to justify its truth or even to advertise or try to convert. Think about it: almost every form of missionary work derives its inner and outer violence from the greed for money and power and, as a result, from the unconscious, shameful insight of the soul that it is selling hot air, in the truest sense of the word.

How can that be? So the Spanish missionaries who happily subjugated the supposed "savages" in South America in the name of their religion were in reality ashamed of their deeds? There is truly nothing about this in the history books.

My friend, you cannot hide anything at all from your soul. Not a speck of dust. For it is the gate to your true home. And in that place there is not a single iota of room for lies. But shedding light onto the connection between objective perception, shame and violence – well, we'll come to that later.

Back to True Religion: its task is to awaken in man that which is true, which he has forgotten. When True Religion preaches, it always shows the way to love and sincerity, to the courage to take responsibility for one's own actions, to true togetherness and understanding. It would never preach "tolerance", for tolerance merely means to tolerate what is different, what is "other". To tolerate is in almost all cases just another word for "to endure" – thus it can turn into rejection at any second.

True Religion only rarely becomes loud and ringing in its utterances, namely when special circumstances demand special actions because it is a matter of protecting real harmony.

True Religion is like wonderful music which delights in ears that can hear. Like a wonderful dinner that delights in discerning tongues that can truly enjoy it. Like a wonderful sunrise rejoicing in eyes that can see. Like the most delicate rose scent, like the most gentle touch.

Fred is silent now. He has spoken the last words wistfully, with melancholy in his voice. Like a former gardener who dreams of his green paradise while having to toil in a coal mine. Where do these thoughts come from? I chase them away and ask …

So there can't really be such a thing as blasphemy, can there?

Blasphemy? Sacrilege? No, True Religion does not know these terms. Heresy, too, is unknown to it, because True Religion would never fight another doctrine, it knows no "holy warriors", no "pagans", no "unbelievers". Genuine, real dignity is never diminished by disregard or insult. The alleged offence of "blasphemy" was invented by religion pushers in order to stifle all dissent and, above all, suppress independent thinking and to keep the sheep in line.
When you encounter True Religion you can recognize it by these attributes.
As always, the same applies here too: by their fruits you shall know them.

I hear your words, and they clearly ring a bell in my mind. But the fanatical followers of the various religions would at this very moment be convinced that you really are the devil.

You can bet on that! But these people should realize: it is they themselves who have chosen their particular version of religion and made it their light in the darkness. No one else. They may have been born into their faith, shaped by it, influenced, brainwashed, trained and seduced. Nevertheless, it is and remains their personal decision whether they continue to allow a particular version of religion to be their light in the night. It is they themselves who allow and permit and choose. No one else. And if a caricature of "light" seduces them to commit violent acts on other people with different choices of faith because they are convinced that their version of faith demands it of them, then it is about time for them to wake up from their nightmare.

You must always keep this truth in mind: you are not born with a particular religion in your blood. It doesn't hide in your genes. You are offered it from outside, get it imposed on you, get trained in it, see it exemplified day by day. And at all times it is up to you to decide whether to accept the faith, to cultivate it, to let it be considered light in your night.

It.

Is.

Your.

Decision.

Next, ask yourself: "So I have a free choice, then why don't I choose a faith from the world's colorful varieties, that makes me and my surroundings happy? Joyful? Alive? A faith that really lights up the night? And that one day will turn the night into day. A faith that will make my heart blossom until the apparent dividing lines between people can dissolve? Why don't I do that?"

Because again, it is your decision, your choice. No one else decides for you. So you follow the commandments of a faith, no matter how elitist and cynical and stifling they may be? It is your decision.

Hmm, a freedom that probably only very few dare to exercise. Mental taboos cloud people's brains like thick smoke.

If someone is happy with his faith, but without hearing the distinct invitation to progress from faith to knowledge, to enlightenment, then he has no real faith but is a consumer of a permanent sleeping pill.
And if a religion dealer evades your questions or labels you a troublemaker because you want to turn faith into knowledge, you'd better take to your heels. They want to throw you into invisible chains.
And once again on the subject of violence: a religion that incites or justifies overt or covert violence – that is not a religion but a fig leaf, a narcotic for its followers for the pain, fear, and anger experienced very early as a child. Feelings that one did not dare to recognize and express, and above all, feelings that one did not simply send back to those who triggered them – namely loveless, heartless, cold people in the immediate environment.

Let no debt remain outstanding, except the continuing debt to love one another, for whoever loves others has fulfilled the law. The commandments "You shall not commit adultery", "You shall not murder", "You shall not steal", "You shall not covet" (…) are summed up in this one command: "Love your neighbor as yourself." Love does no harm to a neighbor. Therefore love is the fulfillment of the law. (Romans, 13)

Instead of confronting and opposing these tyrants, their actions were glorified and excused directly and indirectly by treating innocent people in the same way. A faith that justifies and exemplifies violence is not faith but violence. Your religion peddlers almost always lived according to the principle: "Love your neighbor – provided that he thinks and acts as we see fit, and provided that he has the right skin color, sexual orientation, political views."

Genuine faith is an instrument to acquire knowledge. To come to the recognition that we have an immortal soul, that we are all brothers and sisters who should live for nothing other than to learn incessantly, to make each other happy and the world more beautiful every day. Genuine faith dispels the fog that envelops your souls.

Very nicely put… the devil is a poet – who would've thought it. What you say chimes with a feeling that I've always had. One just doesn't express it freely because it is hidden behind taboos. Even outright atheists often have their children baptized, either "because you never know" or because they don't want to expose their kids to pressure from peers or relatives. Group pressure weighs heavily here.

Okay, you're speaking of True Religion – but what can be said about the many "official" faiths? And in particular, why are they so different when they all claim to offer the same thing, after all?

Today's religions? Almost nowhere do you encounter the real thing. Actually, I can call almost all of them my model students. They have long since forgotten their roots, and at best they offer a pleasant sense of "us and the rest of the world", accompanied by comforting, but meaningless rituals and routines, a seemingly safe haven of patting each other on the back to confirm that you are "on the right side". At the dark end of the spectrum are brainwashing, openly or subtly exercised coercion, the fomenting of fear, hatred and dependence. Genuine humility is replaced by blind hypocrisy. I haven't had much work with them for a long time. As I said, a "religion" or sect that justifies and exemplifies violence – whether physical, mental or spiritual – is not religion but tyranny, most savagely practiced where religious leaders are more powerful than elected governments.

Let there be
no compulsion in religion:
Truth stands out clear
from Error.
(Qu'ran, Al Baqara, Verse 256)

Hmmm, a question about violence: didn't Jesus also use violence when he cleansed the temple of all the shady activities?

You'll have to find the full, complete answer to that question yourself. But maybe there's this much to be said now: "Holy Wrath" does exist. When you throw out miserable bastards who have occupied your house and exploited your good nature, that is not violence. "Always turn the other cheek" is utter nonsense and an invitation to all the parasites and exploiters of this world to pursue their dirty craft undisturbed.

Makes sense, this subtle difference.

With regard to this subject, keep in mind that it is actually a form of violence when you are eyed disapprovingly because you were not in church last Sunday. Or if you look at the woman from the church choir with scorn because she does not want to clean the church "voluntarily", or at the poor parishioner because he does not throw anything into the collection box. This kind of violence is even more effective and hurtful because it is almost impossible to defend oneself against it. Mental or spiritual violence is almost always more despicable than physical violence.

Just meditate on this for once: imagine a pastor who is genuinely happy when you visit him again after a three-year "break", who asks with compassion how you and your loved ones have fared. And now think of a priest who makes an ironic remark to your wife because you have already skipped church twice. Looking at these two scenes, how do you feel?

That I can tell you right away! Even as a teenager, I far preferred to have an honest fight than to be deviously harassed with irony and cynicism. And the hypocrisy with which one succumbed to subliminal blackmail … at baptisms "because of the relatives", at weddings "because otherwise one loses face", at church festivals in traditional costume, at Christmas midnight masses – I always felt extremely uncomfortable with all of this. Today even superficial small talk gets to me in minutes.

Well, you should struggle to overcome that, my friend, if need be for hours on end and with a happy face. Because this ability is an integral part of a successful double life. We'll have to talk about that later. But now I repeat: never and under no circumstances has true

religiosity anything to do with violence. Where there is violence, there is no religion, that is the law of nature. To be sure: defending yourself or other people against violence is not violence.
The violence of religious fanatics is, without exception, a violation of everything which the founders and saints of any given religion lived, taught and died for. The religion of violent fanatics is just an outer shell to more or less successfully distract from their true motives: from fears, powerlessness, greed for power, greed for money. Genuine and healthy missionary work and conversion can only happen through personal example, never through active influence. A quick change of topic now: I must also mention that it was my work to persuade church leaders to install the "indissolubility" of marriage.

Oh dear, key term "divorce rate"!

"What therefore Buddy hath joined together, let no man put asunder " – indirectly this dictum is my work. And yet I have to say this: the intimate bond between two individual souls does exist. It can last many thousands of years, and often the two meet on earth as well, recognize each other and fulfil their tasks together, more often than not as a married couple, but that is not a prerequisite. For couples like these, for these two souls to receive the routine and tired blessing of a frozen,

ossified church or religion is utterly superfluous. If on the other hand they adapt to the cultural customs of time and place and marry, then it is for reasons other than what you would expect. They mostly try then to blend in with their environment to remain in hiding as it were and to pursue their vocation or calling undisturbed. In a way, they lead a double life like secret agents, but for the benefit of all concerned.
What do you think? How many married couples would break up if there were no disadvantages as a consequence, neither materially nor for the children from the marriage nor in terms of personal "reputation"?

Hmmm, that might be an incredibly high number.

What man urgently needs is this: more time to rejoice in nature, simplifying his life and giving up all imagined necessities; more time to rejoice in what he actually needs for life, getting to know his children and friends better, and, most of all, himself and Buddy, who has created him to see. (Yogananda)

Right. Marriage was and is in the strong interest of patriarchy as a place of exploitation and oppression of women and especially of children who are kindly expected to pass on this way of life later on. For many women, it is a cage filled with quiet despair. "It's no use anyway!" – this is a sentence you will often hear from the downcast who shy away from stepping into freedom.

In the course of my life I have met many women and men who have been living happily together for years or even decades, and then got married at some point. For many of them, that was a logical step in mutual harmony, but for just as many it all went rapidly downhill until nothing remained of their original love and respect.

Sometimes, my friend, there's only one solution here that is successful in the long run: you have to leave the places where this kind of brainwashing and enslavement is practiced. Waiting and hoping for partners to change, for religions to change and for them to return to their original tasks – that's almost always a waste of time. A waste of your time – which would be wonderfully invested in thinking, acting and loving on your own. That's what Buddy is patiently waiting for.
Sometimes the courageous step is to leave your familiar surroundings and start completely anew. And not just for self-protection, but because you have the responsibility to use your powers intelligently and economically so that you can become useful to people who depend upon your help and encouragement.

Not for the first time in this crazy conversation, a kind of dizziness takes hold of me. Instinctively, I hold on to my bar stool.

I can see that this is little bit much for you for now, but you're doing fine. We can always come back to this issue if necessary.

Well, a short break would be nice. Maybe another espresso …

May I “torture” you for just a second further on the subject of religion?

I don't mind, I can handle it.

Communion with Buddy, cultivating the friendship with her, everyday life with her – that is the most intimate and absolutely confidential affair a person can have. Not a single other human being is entitled or justified or authorized to interfere, to advise, to dictate, to command. And not a single other human being has the right and only very rarely the possibility to look deeply into the relationship between you and Buddy. There is no room for judgment, condemnation, criticism. If there is such a thing as “sin” on this earth, it would be this one: that heartless armies of religion pushers have withheld this simple truth from you over the millennia.

Small wonder, my friend! They would be out of their jobs in a jiffy!
Of course, there are places on earth where getting to know and coming together with Buddy is a little easier than, say, on Times Square in New York. In rare cases, that can even be a chapel or a church.
But most of the time it is a place outside in peaceful natural surroundings, by a rock, a forest path, a forest clearing, a creek, or alone on an ocean beach. And those who have finally rediscovered Buddy as a their constant companion will walk hand in hand with her even in the middle of Times Square at lunchtime.

Even if I don't quite grasp your meaning yet, it lets a feeling of relief arise in me …

A question for you: "In the name of the Father, the Son and the Holy Spirit" – what's wrong with this formula?

Now we're getting down to the nitty-gritty. I really don't know …

I do. Because I made sure that the formula was shortened almost exactly 1,500 years ago. Originally, it read "In the name of the Mother and the Father, the Daughter and the Son and the Holy Spirit." And even earlier: "In the name of Buddy and the Holy Spirit". Take this home with you to mull over for a bit.

I promise! I think that for many readers the subject of religion will be a wake-up call and perhaps help to make a difference in their lives for the better.
But can we talk a little bit more about something else now? We've already briefly mentioned the children and how from early on their path is blocked from remembering their real calling and discovering the meaning of it all. That's a major concern for me, as a father of teenagers. As a normal person, what can I do to avoid blocking their path if I myself am too scared to take the plunge?

Countless parents have responded to my suggestions and intimations and have become masters at violating the genuine and true human dignity of their children, supposedly for the best educational reasons and with the best intentions.
Let's look at an apparently insignificant example - one that stands for almost every mistake parents can make. I am talking about the habit of not knocking before entering children's rooms. Which is the exact same as not waiting for a "Come in!" or "Stay away!" or silence after knocking.
In many countries parents still do this even after their children have passed the age of 40 and are visiting with their life partner. I state categorically: This is a direct assault on the peace of mind and dignity of the child. Children sense correctly that there is also a fundamental disregard for their personality implied. The instigation to behave like this as parents – self-righteously and

without a guilty conscience – has been one of my most successful incentives.

I remember! I hated that so much that I even bought a padlock with my allowance once. At first, my parents were taken aback, but after a lengthy discussion they accepted my "educational measure". But I know from pals and girlfriends that their parents would have kicked the door in, often with the claim: "It's in your best interests, darling".

I know this sentence well; you often hear it when an absurd or egoistic order is bolstered with this fake justification. Let's take a closer look at this example. How do most younger children deal with it? They allow themselves to be hurt despite a vague, uncomfortable feeling. After all, the child does not want the beloved parents to be "bad", and at the same time wants to be loved unconditionally. So he justifies his parents´ action in his mind as "normal", and quickly puts a lid on the natural reaction to the humiliation.

Do not allow anyone to call you sinners.
You are all Buddy's children,
for he has created you in his image.
It is the greatest sin against yourselves to deny this image. Bring a candle into a cave that has been plunged into darkness for thousands of years, and the darkness will disappear as if it had never existed. It is quite similar with your weaknesses. No matter what they are, as soon as you light the light of goodness, they no longer belong to you.
(Yogananda)

It is important to look at the mechanism that is now developing. It starts in the same way with most other violations of human dignity by parents – beating, locking the child up, silent treatment, ignoring, etc. There is a slow build-up, an atmosphere of permanent and veiled tension, of constant *stress,* because the child can never again rely on his or her room being a safe haven, a secure place of peace and relaxation. The thresholds of irritability are lowered, outbursts "out of the blue" become more frequent, a vicious circle forms because parents and child no longer talk to each other freely.

How I have loved these vicious circles! Because later there was no more work involved with what had been set in motion. Stopping a vicious circle by yourself, on your own, is a sublime art form.

That's been my experience as well! By the way: I once read that every vicious circle has a small, often completely inconspicuous "key point" where it can be broken up and dissolved. The writer Carlos Castaneda, for example, wanted to quit smoking, but he just couldn't manage it. His mentor Don Juan then called his attention to the key point in his case – his shirts with breast pockets in which he kept cigarette packs tucked away. Once he started wearing shirts without breast pockets, he was able to stop the smoking ritual.

Good example, and maybe interesting for some of your readers. But let's move on. A child who has suffered abuse tends to gradually persuade itself later in life that: "My parents' behavior was justified and it made me fit for life," instead of facing the truth beyond any doubt: "It was a wrong decision to tolerate and endure it. I always had the choice to make the right decision, and I did not do it."

It is always easier to establish the conviction: "They are to blame, they have abused my trust, they have hurt my pride, they have put me into emptiness and coldness", instead of allowing yourself to perceive and feel the reality: "I have allowed my human dignity to be violated. I have acted out of cowardice. I have taken their side. And yet, I always had the choice."

Man, I've read that according to a survey almost half of all parents today find nothing wrong with corporal punishment of their children.

That´s a sign of widespread helplessness, because you achieve nothing with it. Each beating requires energy on the part of the parents, but it takes ten times as much energy to heal the loss of trust. After "treatment" of that kind, two things happen sooner or later in adult life. Firstly, the child's inviolable human dignity is unconsciously ashamed of itself because the parents were not put in their place, and secondly, as a form of self-protection, one begins to justify and gloss over one's own cowardice, as something having been "good and right and appropriate". With the supposedly best argument in one's mind: "Think about all the bad things that would have happened to you if you had resisted them." What does this lead to? What do you think?

Well, I think that's obvious. If I sanction my parents' behavior in retrospect, chances are that I'll treat my own children the same way because I have convinced myself that it was right. At least I've sometimes found myself treating my children just as thoughtlessly as my own parents did. Those were very frightening experiences.

Correct, the candidate has top marks again! And with that you have created a vicious circle that will continue to have an effect far into future generations. You feel you are right when you treat your own children the way you were treated. In reality, however, you are protecting yourself so that you no longer feel the pain that your parents inflicted on you. So the crucial point is: If you could clearly recognize that you have inflicted pain on your own children in a completely unjustified way, then you would also immediately understand what your own parents did to you. And right away you could stop making the same mistakes in the future. You would then have to do something to return this baggage to the people who burdened you with it – in whatever way. First and foremost, to regain your lost self-respect.

Oh boy, I guess that explains why family holidays trigger conflicting sentiments in people. "The holier the season, the nastier the people," that's a saying from my wife's home country. But I think healing lies right around the corner. Namely, to dare to take the step towards self-responsibility on one's own or with the help of real friends. This step, I guess, is only possible by taking a good look at yourself in the mirror and realizing that long ago you said "yes" to people who deserved a "no". There are probably many ways to release this burden though, aren't there? There must be, because often the tormentors have died by the time you finally dare to face the truth.

The three most difficult things for a person are not physical peak performances or spiritual showpieces, but first: to repay hate with love; second: to include the excluded; third: to admit that one was wrong. If a person masters these three things, he has mastered life. (Anthony de Mello)

Absolutely, no problem, you can even accomplish it in your mind, for example by writing down everything you've experienced and want to get rid of, and then throwing your lines into a river. Super method. Burying or burning a diary works, too. Excellent devil hacks. In any case more effective than ten years of psychotherapy. One thing I wanted to comment on: whenever self-justification is at work – one of your worst and, for me, most useful inclinations – , whenever you search for someone else to blame, when you yourself are the cause, I was there helping, because then I set a wheel in motion that later saved me the trouble of leading the following generations astray. The old saying goes: "There's only one person worse than the one who is complaining, and that's the one who is justifying himself."

But self-justification is a popular pastime, after all, and in many situations people are even actively invited to do so, for example when someone is summoned to court to stand trial. You can even expect to receive a higher penalty if you don't justify yourself.

Yes, that's why it can be important to consciously lead a double life if you want to get along in this world, at least to some extent.

You mean, "howling with the wolves" is sometimes a good idea?

Absolutely. But it must be done consciously and with common sense, otherwise it is just a helpless strategy to avoid necessary conflicts. You should never lose sight of this: always looking for someone to blame when there is a problem is a slippery slope into mental paralysis. Why? Because every "turning wrong into right", (which is the Latin meaning of the word justification) is a hidden guarantee to repeat the same mistake next time because, after all, it was a "just cause", it was not a mistake. As already stated: looking for people to blame and justifying one's own actions is the surest way to starve and erode your birthright, free will, and to distance yourselves from the truth, namely, that at all times you have the freedom to decide what path you take.

For many readers, this certainly explains the uneasy feeling you get when you've somehow screwed up, and then tried to explain why it happened.

Whenever someone said, "Oh bummer, I made a mistake. I'm sorry. Let's find a solution together to make sure it doesn't happen again," I had to intervene and sometimes work really hard to lead that person back onto the slippery slope.

But your blame culture is working quite smoothly today. And not for nothing do you have umpteen lawyers. Why? Because I have been successful in convincing you that for every problem, every ailment, every mishap, every accident, every loss, whether physical or emotional, there is someone responsible, someone who is to blame – and that is never you yourself!

I am not doing well … the solution is outside of myself.

I shoot myself in the foot … The manufacturer of the gun is to blame.

I burn my tongue on hot coffee ... I sue the coffee shop for a million dollars in damages, because one hundred thousand dollars will be paid out of court in any case.

I feel bad, so inevitably someone else or something "other" has broken its promise! For this conviction to develop deep roots, my friend, was one of my secret operations!

Blame culture, well put. Oprah Winfrey was sued by the meat industry because she casually remarked on her show that, from now on, she would never eat meat again. She was sued because the meat industry's sales dropped sharply nationwide as a result. She almost lost her case.

Yes, today people automatically look for someone to blame. Whoever pretends to know the imaginary or real culprits, whoever pretends to eradicate them, to hold them accountable – that person stands a good chance as a politician. See Trump. Much better chance, at any rate, than a really good person who would offer you the most effective help, namely help towards self-help: Jesus, Gandhi, Dag Hammarskjöld and many others who could have helped you. "Put your own house in order!" – this truth doesn't win elections.
Just take a look at this country: the USA has forgotten that the Declaration of Independence guarantees all citizens the "pursuit of happiness" – but not happiness itself. True happiness is always an almost automatic consequence of something else. To make sure this "something else" is forgotten, that was also my task. This "something else" has to do with self-responsibility, among many other elements – and almost nowhere in the world is this "something else" invited to the dining

table. This "something else" can be found in small, inconspicuous things that, on top of everything, hardly ever cost anything.

In other words: one of my greatest achievements was to seduce you into attributing your alleged happiness to things outside of you. "If only I could accomplish / achieve / obtain this and that, then I'd be happy." Almost all of you have completely overlooked what happens when you are successful with this way of thinking. Have you ever thought about what this might be?

Well, that's obvious, isn't it? At the same time as I achieve something, I'm burdening myself with the fear that I might lose what my happiness now depends on. But I admit that I realized this before I was able to put it into practice in my everyday life.

You do not disappoint me. Make your happiness dependent on something or someone outside of yourself and your soul, and you automatically and inevitably have to take with you as your traveling companion the fear of losing that something again. The object and the fear are two sides of the same coin. This kind of happiness is not happiness at all.

A possible devil hack here: **Realize that you cannot strive for happiness. It is an automatic consequence of something else and not a thing in itself.**

I could hazard a guess here, but your explanation would interest me now. What is happiness the consequence of?

Oh, for how many millennia have I tried to hide this truth from you! Happiness comes when you have found your vocation, your calling, when you have discovered what brings real peace of mind – whether as a baker, mechanic, writer, translator, taxi driver, housewife, doctor.

That has another positive side effect: you gradually become immune to the tyranny of "hurt feelings". This rampant epidemic among you, namely, that you have to take every "hurt feeling" seriously, is one of the most dangerous developments for you in recent decades, and it is almost as bad as your erroneously labelled "political correctness".

What do you think is wrong with that? I know how I personally feel about it, and sometimes I could puke because in most cases political correctness means nothing but dishonesty and outright lying.

When a child is screaming at the top of her lungs because she was not allowed to drink half a gallon of sugared soda pop at once, you have "hurt her feelings". If someone behaves idiotically, and you say to him: "Man, that was really stupid!", then you have hurt his feelings, right? If you call someone a sucker or jerk, and he reacts without expressing any hurt feelings at all but rather says: "Oops, you're right, that was not okay" – what has changed all of a sudden?

What do you have to fear? Nothing.
Who do you have to fear? No one.
Why?
Because the one who allies himself with Buddy enjoys three great benefits: omnipotence without power, exhilaration without wine and life without death. (St. Francis of Assisi)

Well, at least it happens very rarely …

If you call someone an idiot because he's behaved idiotically, and he sues you because you've insulted him, what must have happened to him in the past? What does his thought process look like? Think about it later for yourself. For the moment, I'd like to give you a little hint, that "hurt feelings" are in most cases a conscious or unconscious lie. They almost always arise as a reaction to the expectation that one has a right to something.

But what happens, for example, when a child has just died and the pastor comes to visit, and, instead of giving even a single word of comfort, he demands the unpaid funeral expenses on top of everything – and just five days after the funeral at that! Because that's what happened to a good friend of mine …

That's a good example of when "hurt feelings" are not only justified but are even natural and necessary. And it's also a good example of how "hurt feelings" is a foggy term used to disguise what is really happening within you. There is as much difference between hurt false macho pride and/or self-pity on the one hand, and the response to a real attack on human dignity on the other hand, as there is between Stalin and Gandhi. But you call both "hurt feelings". You even go so far as to abolish losing and winning in school sports among children so as not to burden the tender children's souls. What kind of reality are such little princesses and princes prepared for? What you call "hurt feelings" is in reality almost always a learning experience and not a reason to gun down the apparent culprits, or to take legal action, or to fight the alleged causes. You yourselves are the cause, the culprits. Buddy has given you the wide spectrum of feelings to get to know and live them. It is a law of nature: when you try to numb negative feelings or deny their true causes within you, you will only achieve one thing, namely, to numb all feelings. Your inner emotional universe perishes.

And "political correctness"? You are right, that is almost always a convenient cover-up for lies, at least in the contexts in which it is demanded of you. If, instead, one were to speak of "adhering to basic rules of politeness and consideration", it would have a completely different effect.

I promise I will think about it! But I have to get something off my chest now because I realize the subject of religion still concerns me. Because I've just recalled something from my childhood: in elementary school I suffered a real shock when our religious teacher announced that my little sister was excluded from heaven because she had not yet been baptized! For days, I was totally bewildered until my parents took me out of that class because they were disgusted by this form of indoctrination and hypocrisy. I was obsessed with it for a long time and didn't even believe my parents when they tried to comfort me that there was no original sin, and that Buddy could never be that cruel.

Ah, original sin! As I said before, one of my most ingenious inventions. There is a saying in the Orient: "The little weed is easy to pluck. Give it some time, and not even a crane will be able to do it." I planted this tiny seed, and in a short time it became one of the most effective invisible shackles for the sheep. Add to this false pride and pigheadedness and thus the invention of original sin is kept alive for thousands of years. I invented the fiction of "original sin" for a specific reason. Can you guess why?

Because fear is one of your best allies?

Five out of ten points. My most important goal was to make sure that this fixed idea would push free will and self-responsibility more and more to the sidelines. "I was born evil? So then I don't have to get to the bottom of the true source of my negative inclinations and feelings. And, consequently, I cannot change."
It was then easy for your religion pushers to convince you that even questioning the existence of original sin would be a sin in itself. To this day, this game tempts you to ignore all successful strategies for defeating evil. You don't weaken evil by fighting it – and certainly not by being convinced that it is an "innate element" of human nature. The opposite is true. It is by no means part of your nature; evil is a symptom of a deficiency, a kind of disease. But the phenomenal false pride of your psychologists, ethnologists, sociologists and other "-ologists" does not open the door to this insight. Truly, false pride has been one of my best allies.

How's that? But I can guess why …

How happy am I?
That is the most important question in life for us.
For us people of the First Nations, success does not depend on how much we earn or what social position we occupy, but solely on how happy we are. (Blue Spruce, Native American Pueblo)

Well, simply imagine an old gold miner who's bought a small gold mine with the last of his money. It has been almost fully exploited, but he is obsessed with the conviction that there is still treasure to be found. The more he digs, the deeper he digs, the more convinced he feels that he has just one or two more shovelfuls to work, then he'll have found his heart's desire and be redeemed. He digs and digs, deeper and deeper. What do you think the odds are that, after twenty years, he comes to the surface, takes a deep breath and says: "Well, I screwed up. I won't find anything here. I'll go and dig somewhere else."

Well, very small. His pride keeps him from admitting the error.

Exactly. And it is exactly this characteristic of you humans that has mostly contributed to making my work easier. Especially men are its victims. For many thousands of years, "spiritual leaders" have been indoctrinating you with destructive thoughts. Because they cloud your brain almost from the very first day of your life, you do not make the liberating decision on your eighteenth birthday: "Hey, I'm in the wrong place, this is barren rock. I'll climb back up to daylight and start over somewhere else." No, you keep on digging like blind moles, and with every day that passes while digging in the dead rock, the probability that you will turn around decreases. But think of it! It would only be a tiny second of decision, a stroke of the pen! Forgive yourself – and you can start over from scratch.

What a beautiful thought!

You have done the same with the knowledge of what your souls actually are, what tasks they have, and the life they lead before birth and after death. Your friend Alberto wanted to desert from a German submarine in 1944 as a sailor, and he almost persuaded the entire crew to join in. Until the Gestapo guy on board shot him. He won *this* round!

I'm shocked, I've got goosebumps all over! The movie "The Boat" gave Alberto nightmares for months, as if he'd been there himself … Even today, nothing scares him more than the "ping!"

of a submarine sonar, when his kids are playing a computer game.

Indeed, Buddy was careful to block almost all memory of your previous incarnations – or "rounds" as we call them. Nevertheless reliable information about the actual circumstances before birth and after death can be obtained in any of your bookstores. Michael Newton is one of the authors who was permitted an insight, and who reported it truthfully.

Hey, what a coincidence! That book was given to me as a birthday present, but I haven't read it yet. "Journey of Souls".

Then it's about time - have fun with it. Maybe I'll have to get back to that topic later on.
Just think about it: what "original sin", what guilt is a baby burdened with, when it's born into a cruel and cold family and then shaken to death by its father because it cries all night? What made it "deserve" a fate like that? Why did the baby soul choose this family? A real answer to these questions is impossible without True Faith and without knowing what True Religion means. Such an attempt would lead straight into a situation completely devoid of joy of life. A peek into any morning newspaper would make you complain about the injustice in the world – independent of the material circumstances in which one lives. Life would lose all

meaning if there was not a life before birth and after death.

That was and is one of my working hypotheses, otherwise I'd actually go crazy just reading the morning paper.

Don't bother. Most of it's only reports about activities I initiated anyway, because good news doesn't rake in new subscribers … Only those who have true faith can get answers that grant lasting peace of mind.
But true faith, my friend, is not taught anywhere; it has to be worked for and earned in the face of all the resistance and contradictions of life. Often my devoted disciples, and all the self-proclaimed spiritual guides and "men of god" showed you the wrong way and found and still find countless followers. Simply because people's longing for meaning and authenticity is so great, and offers to give lasting and real satisfaction of this longing are so few.
This has always been my big break; all sects and cults find their lever and entrance here. They offer counterfeit goods, imitations, and a false sense of peace in response to real and legitimate needs of the soul. There is an old saying: "False gold exists for three reasons: firstly, because of the greed of men; secondly because of their inability to differentiate; and thirdly, because real gold exists."

But that's the crux of the matter here! Who is a born goldsmith? Where can I learn to distinguish between the genuine and the bogus? Wherever you look – the powers that be all try to deny us this very ability, or rather to disable it!

The attempt to falsify is a much stronger weapon than the attempt to destroy. Mankind must always be given the freedom of choice. As soon as a teacher has passed on his work to the world, a distorted version of it must appear – the falsification must come into being so that people can choose between real gold and false gold. (Edward Bach)

Identifying real gold, discovering true faith and correct signposts – you will only gain the ability to discern, if you learn to love yourself. That's one of the best recipes, the best devil hacks against being seduced by me. Those who love themselves do not let themselves go or fall into chronic depression. If you love yourself, you'll be able to see through every person sooner or later. And there is one consolation: behind the smoke screens and humbug of religion there is evidence of the genuine article, as we have already talked about on the subject of True Religion. And just one more thing: every true guide of the soul, every true friend will always remind you that love is the only purpose of life, and your free will is the most important tool to discover and live this love. As I've already said, he or she will never attempt to proselytize, to convert or to persuade – no matter how subtly. My devil hack for you at this point: By their fruits you shall know them. And will you please assume responsibility for every single second of your life!

I'm trying not to get worked up about the countless sects and religions, from Scientology to Jehovah's Witnesses to the state-sanctioned cults. That's a powerful trigger for me.

Don't forget: fighting them only makes them stronger and gives them wings and permission to exist.

I won't forget that anymore, I promise! I'll take a deep breath now and move on to the question: can you please elaborate on the life of the soul after death?

Once again from the beginning? Ok, at almost all times, even during many centuries of Original Christianity and even today, there was and still is the knowledge in many places that each individual soul spends many lives on earth to fulfil certain tasks in any given round – sometimes with more success, sometimes with less. And even if without success – well then, better luck next time!

Start by doing what's necessary,
then do what's possible,
and suddenly you are doing the impossible.
(St. Francis of Assisi)

Hmm, so our body is just a kind of vehicle for the soul, and it gets a new one with every round?

Right, in all colors and shapes and varying amounts of horsepower. From tractors to Ferraris. Depending on the special task in each round.

So "May he or she rest in peace" isn't a very suitable wish at a funeral, is it? How come we know so little about all of this?

Well, first of all, you have established a scientific method that is blind in more than one eye. And secondly, it is indeed my achievement. One day, at a gathering about 1,300 years ago, I celebrated one of my greatest successes. I managed to seduce the then "pastors" of the Christian Catholic Church to throw out an essential item of their credo and arbitrarily spread new doctrines. What they chose to dispense with was the knowledge of the transmigration of the soul. With one selfish stroke of the pen, they abolished the article

of faith that every human being has an immortal soul which returns to earth again and again.
I suggested a new theory to these church leaders at that time: "If we preach from now on that this present life on earth is the only possible life, then our flocks of sheep will make all the more effort to behave, here and now, in a godly manner in order to enter Paradise." They believed that this way they could banish the thought: "This time I'll let it all hang out because I can make up for it in the next life." Truly, the church elders were completely wrong about human nature and my task as well, my friend. Back then, as now, it's much easier for me to convince you that "A godly life full of self-discipline is far too exhausting and boring. I might as well give up trying and just believe in nothing at all. And should Buddy indeed exist, somehow things will turn out for the best after I'm gone."

When I look around my circle of acquaintances and when I consider what the media and science promulgate as "normal", that sounds more than plausible.

Back then, the priests also misjudged something else, namely, what happens when you preach empty convictions instead of the truth. The unconscious part of the human being, the eye of the soul, perceives the lie and falls into spiritual distress, which the church has not been able to heal to this day. However the sharp eyes of the many clairvoyants and the spiritually gifted had retained a direct insight into the true life of the soul and were able to expose the false doctrine of the church representatives.

Yes, exactly, and if they did not keep their mouths shut, they often found their lives shortened in not very pleasant ways…

The church fathers pushed the instinctive knowledge of "karma" into the spiritual "underground" – the knowledge that everything I send out comes back to me. Whatever I give comes back. The good as well as the evil. If not immediately, then later, perhaps a thousand years later. The new doctrine was therefore not so difficult to instill, because then as now, the sometimes considerable time lag until something "returns to me" is probably the biggest obstacle to recognizing that man himself attracts everything quasi-magnetically, or freely chooses what happens to him.

Well, it's probably the same as with the wrong diet: sometimes it takes years or decades until I reap what I have sown ...

Good example. Humankind also has lost sight of the fact that karma works on a large scale as well. When a group, a city or a whole country attacks and exploits other communities or states, then that will return as well – even to the good people in the attacking country. The only remedy on a collective level would be for the offending country to actively initiate a process of repentance and reconciliation.

Well, then many countries in the world have a lot of catching up to do, don't they? It strikes me that a core article of Christian teachings is based on lies!

Yep, didn't I do well? Such big and credible lies were spread so that, even today, people still blow themselves up and wage wars, not just out of childish vanity and insatiable greed, but also in the name of Buddy! As if our best friend would have wanted that! Does anyone believe that a murdering "holy warrior" or his instigators just die, and then that's it? Don't they perhaps reap some of what they have sown, after all?

So there is indeed such a thing as justice in all that chaos?

This is an important question to which each of you will have to find your own answers in the course of your lives. Independent and uninfluenced answers. Even if they are answers that do not please your immediate environment because the "normal" and "accepted" answers look different for the moment.
Actually a strange fact should whisper something very clearly into your ear, namely, that centuries ago catholic priests chose an old Roman instrument of torture as

their new symbol – instead of what would be much more appropriate, a symbol representing resurrection, love and joy. Just a century later, the Romans decided to let the gallows do the work instead of the cross.

Oops, I think only very few people who have a cross hanging from a chain around their neck are aware of that. Would they have chosen a gallows noose as well?

Interesting thought.

Something that has always irritated and annoyed me is the brainwashing by the Catholic Church, to the extent that the Vatican determines, year after year, the Bible texts to be used for sermons etc. Sunday after Sunday. Although the Bible does have hundreds of optimistic passages celebrating love, their self-proclaimed supremo chooses almost exclusively depressing topics emphasizing the perpetual struggle against sin, glorifying suffering and hardship. And when love and joyfulness occur, then only as a distant goal and prize in paradise.
Or look at the joyless, cold texts with which one says goodbye in obituaries, particularly those of women. There is usually talk of "life endured with devotion, full of work". One almost never says "thank you" to a person because he brought joy and laughter to his people. Religions present burdens, toil and pain as key to getting to heaven. But what the proclaimers of such idiocy have perpetrated themselves behind walls and closed doors, this comes to light only gradually. And we still allow babies to be baptized, for

the sole reason that otherwise family or neighbors might give looks of disapproval …

Think about the following question, take your time with it: what would happen if during the service you kissed your girlfriend with all your heart in a church, mosque, synagogue, or temple anywhere in the world? What would happen if you showed clearly in front of everyone that you loved your partner dearly? And what would happen if two men or two women did the same? How many of your bishops and popes and mullahs and priest are people who really radiate joy of life and love for humanity – people with whom you immediately get the feeling that this is how you want to be as well?

Again it comes down to the fruits by which you're supposed to recognize them.

I'll tell you, one of my greatest challenges in the past was to hide Buddy in such a way that she was hardly ever likely to be at home exactly where she was being worshipped. How about a little anecdote on the side? My friend Jesus once walked past a church in the south of this country here when he saw a man whose earthly body robe was painted deep black, and who was sitting on the steps of a small church. Jesus asked him why he was so sad. He replied: "I would so much like to pray inside the church, but that is not allowed for people like me." Jesus said to him: "Never mind, I'm not allowed in, either."

I know the story, but in the context of our conversation it makes even more sense. Your "friend" Jesus? I can't quite wrap my mind around that yet.

Well, my friend, it should gradually become more and more obvious to you that I was personally assigned and sent out by Buddy to help you play hide and seek. I know, your religion dealers sold you the fairy tale that I am an opponent of Buddy. Ridiculous! You can't drive a wedge between Buddy and any atom in the universe. You and me, Buddy and you, the universe and you and me – we are one. The fragmentation into diversity happens solely in your head – and I was its engine, that was the idea. In the structure of everything, I am the breaker, the fragmenter.

An important question comes to mind. Many of us have the greatest difficulties in even turning to spirituality and believing in something higher, because they keep asking themselves: "Why does Buddy allow so much suffering in the world?" I myself can guess what's going on, but I can't put my feeling about it into words.

The most important hour is always the present, the most significant person is precisely the one sitting across from you right now; the most necessary work is always love. (Meister Eckhart)

That is one of the oldest questions of mankind. I've already given the answer, but Yogananda is right on target:

"All suffering comes from the abuse of free will. Buddy has bestowed on us the ability to accept or reject free will. It is not her will that we suffer pain; but she does not intervene when we decide to take action that brings us pain and suffering.

People do not heed the wise counsel of the saints but expect to be saved by unusual circumstances or some miracle when they are in need or distress. Buddy can accomplish everything, but she knows that love and the right behavior of man cannot be bought with miracles.

Buddy has sent us out as her children, and as such we must return to her again. There is only one way to reunite with her: to use your own will. No other force or power on earth or in heaven can do this for us. But if you call for Buddy from the bottom of

your heart, she will send you teachers who will lead you home from the wasteland of pain to the house of her eternal joy.
Buddy has bestowed on you free will and thus cannot act like a dictator. Although she possesses omnipotence, she will not simply free you from your suffering if you have chosen the wrong course of action. Is it right to expect her to free you from all burdens if you constantly violate her laws with your thoughts and actions? Follow her principles, as Jesus laid them down in the Sermon on the Mount; therein lies the secret of happiness."

This was written by Yogananda, one of your best friends. A very effective devil hack is reading his books, particularly the "Autobiography of a Yogi" and "Where there is Light". In fact, the suffering in the world can only be explained when one has true faith – regardless of the name of the religion from which you want to obtain wisdom, inspiration and confidence.
Without the certainty that every soul experiences justice, there is no answer to the question about meaning. Without the absolute certainty that there is free will, there is none, either.

I'm not unfamiliar with Yogananda's work. I found it so timelessly valid and authentic that I even inspired my son to participate in a youth camp organized by his contemporary followers. Unfortunately, that backfired completely because it seems that Yogananda's modern followers have strayed somewhat from the openness and love that characterized his work.

I know about this and it only confirms a law of nature. There is a little anecdote about a famous twelfth-century spiritual teacher who was sick in bed and one day received a visit from an equally sublime master. That master asked him if he had a special wish. "An apple would be nice," said the sick teacher, even though it was in the midst of winter. The visitor raised his hand vertically upwards, and when he let it sink again, he had an apple in his hand which he handed to the patient. A little later, when the visitor was on his way back home, the student who had accompanied him asked: "Master, I couldn't help but notice that the apple had a wormhole. Forgive me the question, but how can it be that a fruit from the celestial sphere was afflicted with such a flaw?" – "My faithful friend, without exception everything that comes into contact with the earthly realm must share in its imperfection."

No holy man, no real guru or master can guard against his followers' distorting his message, misunderstanding it, or destroying it out of selfishness or stupidity. On the contrary, as I said before, this is a law of nature. The Inquisition had nothing to do with Jesus's message. Read the Sermon on the Mount, and you can clearly see what's going on.

Got it, I was just a bit put off by Yogananda´s current students. Back to the previous topic of the fate of the soul. So you're telling me in plain English that a baby murdered by its father chose this path himself before he was born? On the one hand, that's a pretty horrible thought, but on the other hand, I think there is some comfort in that …

Once again, in other words: in order for everything to become meaningful, even all the wild stuff filling the morning papers, you need the rock-solid conviction that every human being has chosen his or her path on this earth, with all its experiences and events, long before birth – in order to learn and mature and to evolve his or her soul. And, of course, also to postpone some of these self-chosen lessons and to take the occasional detour. To create this conviction for yourself would have many advantages.
By the way: your religious traders have worked hard throughout history to hide the true connections between cause and effect.

But why?

To cement their own power. They have simply turned nearly every misfortune into a "punishment by God", or into an expression of "Buddy´s will". And then they talked you into believing that only they knew how to regain Buddy's mercy: of course, by submitting to their instructions and insights and rituals. In this way, they prevented your recognizing true cause-and-effect. If an illness is " Buddy's punishment" I don't have to find out what really caused it and how to heal it but rather sacrifice a goat and fill a collection bag in church.

Okay, now I see a little more clearly. As for the soul's journeys through many lifetimes: many people are absolutely convinced that there is no life after death. And certainly no return of the souls. How do you answer them?

"Well, well, if that is your opinion," I say and leave them alone, because that conviction used to play into my hands, after all. To soften it up and escape its numbing influence, there is a secret super devil hack:
If someone believes something but does not know, he should always ask himself: "Why do I believe this? What consequences does it have in my everyday life? What exactly does it benefit me and others in view of the fact that I only believe and do not yet know?"
In essence, every belief, dogma or doctrine actually means *"not knowing something"*. It is merely a working hypothesis waiting for verification. As said before, beliefs, dogmas and doctrines are always an intermediate stage, a friendly invitation to embark on the path to knowledge. "Why do I believe what I

believe?" – *this* question is one of the keys to happiness, as inconspicuous as it may seem.

But in many religions faith is the iron law, the unconditional foundation! Expressing doubts can cost you your head!

Right, and the foundation for what? What kind of house would you like to build on it? If you have the unquestioned belief that a trip around the world, a new profession, a certain person will bring you happiness in life, do you then go to a very large house once a week, kneel down, say a few words and wait for someone to carry you around the world, to give you a doctor's degree without any effort, or for your beloved to consider you her soulmate? Faith is a step on a path that ends with knowledge. If someone wants to convince you that faith alone is the final step, then he is like a fitness trainer who makes you believe that your muscles are being trained just by watching his videos. An ancient proverb, somewhat adapted to our time, says: "Trust in Buddy, but have your car lubricated in time." And don't ever listen to people who want to convince you that you can't know, and therefore faith and "confidence in paradise" are absolutely necessary, of course plus the whole package of rituals and dogmas around faith. They are like blind people who want to make you believe that "eyesight" is an invention of the devil. Funny, isn't it? Okay, ready for a change of topic?

I think so, there's already so much food for thought for me and the readers.

Good, because there are still a few more topics in need of my attention, for example *music.*

Music? What about it?

If there is to be peace in the world,
there must be peace in the nations.
If there is to be peace in the nations,
there must be peace in the cities.
If there is to be peace in the cities,
there must be peace between neighbors.
If there is to be peace between neighbors,
there must be peace in the home.
If there is to be peace in the home,
there must be peace in the heart.
(Lao Tzu)

Music has long been one of my biggest problems, because a natural access to Buddy is hidden in it, as with certain forms of meditation, the art of singing, and being in contact with nature. People have always felt and acted on this as well. But then we drip fed you texts, notes and beats that closed this channel again to a great extent.

Texts and beats?

Just sit down with a pair of headphones and compare Beethoven's sixth symphony with military music, rap music, heavy metal and the like. Listen and feel the difference. To call both "music" is like labeling Romeo and Juliet´s feelings for each other and the greed for a hamburger with the word "love". Today's music is largely numbing instead of awakening – a flattening of feeling, the cementing of differences, of racism, contempt for women, contempt for non-members, for "others" and so on. Almost as effective as preaching in a Catholic church.

Oh dear, but love is serenaded just about everywhere: "All you need is love!"

Right, it sounds like a contradiction, but it's not. I'll leave it up to you to resolve it. Just consider the difference between tender, harmonious, cosmic sexuality which lifts the partners into higher spiritual spheres, on the one hand, and pornography on the other. And then take your time to hear what the lyrics to the theme "I love you!" actually say. And how often you stumble upon self-pity, obsession, bondage and control addiction, but you rarely encounter unconditional love.

Okay, I'll take a deep breath for now and concentrate. Let´s take a short break.

> *For a few seconds I close my eyes and look, almost a little amused, at the whirl of thoughts and feelings that the conversation has triggered in me. Then I notice that I'm looking at the chaos from the outside, as if I'm not creating the thoughts myself. Strange. I feel like a zoo visitor in front of the monkey cage … until curiosity gains the upper hand.*

I've rather lost sight of what your actual job is. What is its purpose? Perhaps you can explain it to the readers in other words.

But of course. For this, let's go back to religion and its meaning. So our primary task was to distract you from the essentials in life. Everything important and beautiful and fulfilling in life costs nothing. It's absolutely free. We have obscured this truth.

You know, everything is connected with everything else; indeed, everything is everything. Every soul is Buddy playing hide and seek with himself.

The challenge for me was to make this apparent separation between Buddy and a soul so perfect that the soul, for the entire duration of its current round, forgets who it is, where it comes from, and what its task on earth is. The amnesia itself is part of Buddy´s game of hide and seek. My task was to make finding her as difficult as possible.

It is said that the devil likes to acquire souls by purchase, entering into a pact with his human business partner. Which of course would make finding Buddy completely impossible.

Buying souls? Well, now you have an idea of what a lie that was, right? To fulfil my task, I had a large arsenal of methods and tools at my disposal. Want one more example? The method by which you are taught to pray in your churches. Praying is indeed an access gate to Mama Buddy, but not the way you've learned it. Because you're always begging like needy creatures who lack something. In this way you're sending an image of yourselves into the world as imperfect beings. The universe inevitably follows your invitation and cements your neediness because you send it out as such into the universe.

Devil hack alarm: praying correctly means that you imagine that the prayer has already been answered. The universe cannot help but accept that invocation. This works best in meditation.

Why? Well, because Buddy has created you in her image! She would never send herself into the world as a have-not and poor beggar. You are her daughters and sons, you are Buddy. Not creatures whining in churches like little children because they are denied something.

Fred, try telling that to my old religion teacher! Okay, in summary: if someone succeeds in severing the contact between Buddy and himself, that is, between Buddy and a soul, then you were at work? So if a priest pretends that contact with Buddy is possible exclusively and only through him or through certain rituals and obedience to his dogmas, then he is playing into your hands? Because if you look closely, he's actually interrupting the direct connection.

That's right. It applies whenever he pretends that without his intercession there is no pathway to Buddy. For this game of hide-and-seek, I was sent out by our best friend, because it's only fun if you can't be found right away. But it´s no fun, either, not being found at all. Remember your childhood? There was nothing more boring when playing hide-and-seek than being found immediately or not being found at all, right? Many true priests and true men and women of god do a successful job undermining my work and actually helping the soul find its way back, but they are few and far between. You can recognize them by the fact that they would never force their faith on you. With such people, you may feel comfortable and accepted unconditionally, whether black or white, yellow or gay, LGBT or any of the colors of the rainbow.

And what about the others? Nothing is more repugnant to the vast majority of them than the physical, mental and spiritual independence of their flocks. Emblematic of this is the fact that the priesthood of all denominations has always cooperated with the powerful and the tyrants, and has even given its blessing to their crimes. Mussolini, Hitler, Franco, Cortez, etc. – many catholic clerics were their obedient helpers or stood passively on the sidelines. Take the trouble to listen to their sermons today when the word "love" comes up in them – which is seldom enough the case. And then pay close attention to the contexts in which it occurs. Their "love" is always contingent because it is connected with terms and conditions. Be good and well-behaved, then you will go to heaven.

Watch your thoughts,
for they become words.
Watch your words,
for they become actions.
Watch your actions, for they become habits.
Watch your habits, for they become character.
Watch your character, for it becomes your destiny.

But Buddy does not set any terms and conditions. Lost sons and daughters can always return. And why shouldn't they? They are Buddy. You are Buddy. By the way, it is a great crime, and not just in this context, to exclude homosexuality, transsexuality and "being different" in general from the social interactions of the "normals" and to confront them with intolerance, callousness and hatred.

I agree wholeheartedly. If these religious criminals could only guess at the damage they do to the minds and souls of those affected, they would spend the rest of their lives recanting.

Yes, it's at those moments that I'm ashamed of my success. One of my most successful tricks was to make celibacy acceptable to the Catholic Church, and to exclude women from the priesthood. Why the religion peddlers adopted these idiotic ideas without resistance and why they thought that it would grant easier access to Buddy is still a mystery to me today. The opposite is the case. A complete human being can help others to become complete themselves. A married man can become a good marriage counselor. A former thief can become a good policeman. Sometimes it's a mystery to me how easily you let yourselves be pushed to believe completely twisted interpretations of the Bible, Quran, and Torah. You let yourselves be trained and drilled to be submissive! Even the Apostle Paul is of the opinion that "bishops should be married and be good fathers of families".

What? Really? Where can that be found in the Bible?

Check it out: 1 Timothy 3:1 to 3:4.

I'll certainly do that!

Good, and take time to ponder over these contexts. Change of subject: may I introduce you to one more of my tools?

Would I want to know about it?

Well, certainly! It's the praise and promotion of patriotism. Basically, it is a good thing to stand up for one's own family, one's own community, for town and country, and to appreciate and defend them. But I managed to introduce another element, and that is what made it so appealing to me. Can you think of what that could be?

Well, I think that putting one's own country before others and protecting it should be somewhat natural and OK.

Well yes, but that is the crucial question: do you really want to protect your country and its people, or do you just want to give the appearance in public and to yourself that you are protecting them?

Suppose your country is faced with a saber-rattling neighboring country led by power-hungry, childish characters who threaten you with war mainly because then they wouldn't have to take up arms themselves. What does "patriotism" mean in that case? To wage war at the expense of the lives of many thousands of your brothers and sisters? Or does it mean to approach the other country peacefully, helping it to help itself, with generous support in all areas, up to and including secretly bribing the corrupt leaders there?

I think it depends on what the motives behind the saber-rattling are. Does the neighboring state want to divert attention from its own problems? Does it want to extend its borders out of a lust for power? Does it want to settle old scores, and is therefore acting out of injured pride?

So what is patriotism? *Actually* doing what is best for your country, or only *apparently* doing what is best? The seemingly best, nourished by the false pride of some fools in governments who abuse the thimble-full of power they got from Buddy? Or *really* doing the best for the good of all? Who is more patriotic, the person joining the military or the conscientious objector?

You have to find good answers to these questions to become immune to my patriotism poison. In any case, it has almost always been easy for me to convince patriots that their false pride, their vanity, are better advisers than reason, cooperation and love for humanity. The Gandhis of this world are the exception. Do you know what my sharpest weapon here was, the perfect foundation?

Let´s hear it!

To instill in you the conviction that there have always been "superior" people and "inferior" people! Your systems for judging people by good and bad, by wallet, intelligence, skin color, fashion taste, body type, gender, religion, sexual orientation, music preferences, etc. – these prejudicial mechanisms are so successful that you have almost completely forgotten the most important message of your true friends today. Jesus, Mohammed, Buddha, Krishna, Meister Eckhart and many others have always reminded you that you are brothers and sisters without exception, sons and daughters of Buddy without exception. And that real strength lies in diversity, not in uniformity. Monotonous, boring uniformity has nothing to do with equality, which is absolutely necessary. That's the only reason why four eyes see more than two!
With every war, you wage war within the family! Every terrorist kills his brother, his sister and himself. You have forgotten how artificial and self-fabricated

apparent separations are, between man and woman, between different skin colors, between rural and urban populations, between North and South, East and West. The superiority of any group of people is just an illusion. Listen carefully, this is important! What do you think? If the baby of a devout Jewish family is mixed up in the hospital with that of a fanatical Muslim family, what will it grow up to be?

I was looking for you from the beginning, and could not find you.
I called out loudly for you from the church tower, from the minaret. I rang the temple bell at sunrise and sunset. In vain I bathed in the Ganges, disappointed I returned from the Kaaba.
I looked for you in the lines of Bible and Torah, of the Quran and the Tao Teh King, in all lines of the world.
I traveled around the globe, flew to the heavens, my beloved.
Only when I looked into my heart, I found you.
(Al Ghazali)

I haven´t thought about that yet. But I suppose it´ll be a devout Muslim?

Right. As I said, to imagine that a religion is anchored somehow in the genes, "in the blood", is pure delusion.

This dogma has as little substance as the idea that one has political convictions, "noble origins" or a "racial consciousness" in one's blood. You alone bear the responsibility for it! To believe such nonsense is your personal decision!

Or do you really believe that a queen´s baby, if it were raised in a peasant family, would automatically grow up to become a little prince? As far as the mental and spiritual development of a person is concerned, almost nothing is anchored in the genes. The claim of your blue-blooded "nobles" that, by birth, a special spiritual privilege is transferred which makes them "higher-value" human beings compared to their subjects – this crackpot idea has colored your history books blood-red since the beginning of time. The truth is: a Christian can consciously decide to transform himself into a Hindu and vice versa. Faith is replaceable, knowledge and experience are not.

Not only with religion but also with the phantasmagoria of "nationalism" and "patriotism", a natural, actually innate, and deeply human yearning is abused, namely the yearning for trust, for real togetherness, for unconditional acceptance, for the feeling of "us". All for one and one for all! Boy, what I had to go through in order to neutralize the positive effect of the novel "The Three Musketeers" on the readers!

I recall the goosebumps I had when I was allowed to watch one of the film adaptations as a child. Perhaps a little info for the readers: the author Alexandre Dumas was of black skin color.

That's good, that will come as a surprise to many of your readers! Yes, instead of living the real core of communion, you turn it into the basis of all opposition and antagonism in the world. "Us here and then those outside the door, beyond the garden fence, the walls, in the other neighborhood, in the other club, in the other country." Us whites here, and all the other skin colors there. Us blacks here, and the evil reds there. Us good guys here, and all the others, the bad guys, there. We the righteous and the "Master Race" here, and all the others, the savages and primitives, there. Us country people here, and the city folks far removed from nature over there. Us clever city folks here, and the country bumpkins there. Indeed, it is often only a small step from the right to live of the "right people" to the denial of that right to the "unfit", which may be eradicated with impunity.

The English have a saying for it: "Give a dog a bad name and then hang it."

Sure, but keep in mind that the saying also works the other way round. "Give a merciless tyrant a good name and make him worthy of worship". You even succeed in hiding from yourselves, or justifying, the cold inhumanity of a tyranny if it bears a special label: "Communism", "Theocracy", "Thousand-Year-Reich", "Liberation Army", and so on.
Never lose sight of the fact that absolutely every neo-Nazi in the world has some Jewish ancestry. Every white supremacist has some African, Indian, East Asian antecedents, just like any other person. "Racial purity" is a sheer illusion to create a pedestal for yourself. There is no racial purity. You are all genuine half-breeds and hybrids, enriched with the genes of all skin colors.
You have to learn that real power lies in diversity! Anyone who uses family, religion, skin color, gender, preferences, philosophy or political convictions to devalue other people, and to consider a certain group more valuable than another, insults Buddy and betrays himself.

Well, seems we still have a lot to learn as citizens of the world.

True, but you can do it.

Maybe the present day awareness of the hidden everyday racism in many parts of the world is a beginning.
Keyword # BlackLivesMatter.

Why should you forgive the people who have done evil to you? Because the moment you strike back in anger you deny your own divine nature – you are then no better than the one who attacked you. But if you reveal your spiritual power, you'll receive great blessings; besides, the power of right conduct helps to clear up the existing misunderstanding, and you bring light into the world. (Yogananda)

You have to take a long-term approach. Division and segregation start at home on a small scale, as when you prefer one child over another because he or she is "better", meaning more obedient and well-behaved. It carries on in the schoolyard, where bullies are secretly admired instead of getting stopped there and then, and it ends with longing for the strong man in politics, who promises to assuage the feelings of weakness and fear in his followers. Wherever there was raw competition, sexism, discrimination, racism, I stood by and rubbed my hands because you were doing my job so well. The devil hack? Learn to listen, learn to understand, and then realize that you are all brothers and sisters.

So you were actually the "dark killer of happiness", if I see it right. But happiness, that's what everyone pursues, right? There must be many who manage to elude you, aren't there?

Well, yes. But the one who is running almost never notices that happiness is constantly following behind. My job in this case was to prevent you from stopping and turning around. I was most successful in doing this by waving substitute gratifications in front of your nose, or fomenting fears that kept you on your toes. The carrot-and-stick approach, after all. I had to prevent you from remembering your true origin, your true task, your true sources of happiness. That wasn't hard. Almost all of you are quickly and easily satisfied with the crumbs on the cold floor in the basement of the House of Truth. Imagine, I have even succeeded in transforming the ancient art of yoga into a sport that publishes its own newspapers and is succumbing to competitive thinking. Yet it could be such a fine gateway to Buddy.

Yes, for the donkey, the thistle is a delicious fruit. I read this saying recently.

That describes it exactly.

If I may say so, it was not very nice of you to lead us on these wild goose chases!

Slow down, my friend! We are coming to a very important point. Because appearances are deceptive. My seductions rarely succeed without the secret consent of the one being seduced. A false guru has a commodity to offer that would have no market if the disciple was not avid for it. This is exactly where the connection, the kinship between seducer and seduced resides. I hardly need to actively intervene, a nudge is enough. It's an exchange of goods. Most of the time the deal looks like this: you give me one pound of attention, appreciation and applause, I give you five pounds of dependence and mental enslavement. Hardly anything weakens the natural rebellious instincts of a slave more than being given a "Slave of the Month" plaque. Or the seducer generously throws around tickets to emotional rollercoasters of tension and relaxation. These are especially popular with the perpetrators because the victims tend to confuse them with authentic learning progress. In the long run, this is always a bad deal for the victim, but almost always happens with the silent consent of all parties involved.

I have learned silence
from the talkative,
tolerance from the intolerant,
and kindness from the unkind.
I shouldn't be ungrateful to these teachers.
(Kahlil Gibran)

As far as happiness, love and especially physical love are concerned, you actually did a great job, even I can see that. Almost nowhere in everyday life can I discover the real thing; the word "love" is used exaggeratedly, interchangeably and arbitrarily. "I love you" and "I love hamburgers". It looks as if you must own many movie and television companies …

You are right: love, sex, physical and emotional attraction – this part of life was one of the great challenges for me, because in them are hidden several ways to escape me and to wake up to your reality and true destiny.

So then it would be a fine devil hack to give more space to love in your own life, to give more space to togetherness, to mindfulness.

The finest hack! What is love? It is like a beacon in the dark night which leads back to the right path to self-realization. Love makes it possible for Buddy´s spark

within you to lead you back to Buddy directly, and it ends the game of hide and seek.
Almost all of you know this clear feeling of the value of love and the longing for it, because it is not by chance that it plays such a huge role in your music, in the media, etc. You don't know what I had to go through in order to redirect this energy, to take away its power and color it dark. From the porn industry all the way to Viagra and competitive thought – you know what I mean: who has the longest, how often can you do it, how many women/men have you had so far, I only love you if you …, the obsessive love for pets, the "love" for certain dishes on your plate, for pastime and hobby, for sports and so on and so forth. The creation of substitute drugs was one of my main activities. Today you refer to many forms of veiled selfishness as "love".

By chance, I read about a case today that shows there is another way. A farmer who had regularly won prizes at agricultural fairs with his crops always shared his best seeds with all the farmers in the neighborhood. When he was asked why, he said: "Out of selfishness. If my neighbors grow inferior crops, cross pollination also reduces the quality of my own plants. That's why I want them to grow only the very best." This really impressed me because it could serve as a parable for so much more.

The man is actually not really the sharpest tool in my box, but didn't he himself say: "out of selfishness"…

Well, with such high standards every action can be called selfish, can't it?

No, what you call egotism is almost always a veiled form of self-harm. Egotism always drives you into isolation, and that is the opposite of what you are meant for and what really makes you happy. Self-love and egotism, those are as different as solar energy and atomic energy. The one heals, the other destroys.

So there's another topic that I'll have to think about. But let's stay with the subject of sex for now …

You're welcome! I am glad you have the courage to do so, because one of my most diabolical moves was intensifying the taboo against talking openly and honestly about sex and all its varieties and shades, let alone the problems you have with it.
After all, what is the physical union when you look at it in detail? Two people play the musical instruments of their bodies and sexual organs so happily and in harmony that something new, something alive, is created. New sounds, never heard before, almost every time a new music which makes the surroundings vibrate for miles around. And dance. From a simple inspiring chord all the way to a small symphony. Like good music, like harmonious dancing, it's a source of joy, pleasure,

optimism, and inspiration for great deeds. It is truly good medicine, it prevents, heals, strengthens, makes invulnerable, acts as an ideal antidepressant. Sex brings color where grey used to prevail, brings truth to the light of day. Brings clarity where fog clouded the view. And all of that without a dime of expense, except perhaps for condoms. Do you have any idea how hard it was for me to drag sex down into the swamp of forgetting everything that real pleasure, real happiness means? But I did it!

You only have to look at magazine covers in newsagents to see how successful your methods are.

Yes, comparison and competitive thinking, the inability to stay engaged with the present moment, nutrition that numbs the senses, pornography. And above all the dead weight of archaic religious ideas. Not forgetting your "sexperts" who talk nonsense like "the sex drive usually declines with age". That's like tying crutches to someone's legs and then discovering that he walks more slowly than before. Consequently many of you are either afraid of sex or sometimes prefer an ice cream with three scoops over the cheerful dance in bed because there's hardly any difference in the emotional experience.
And we've already talked about this: my most successful helpers were the religions that made two things out of

sex: something dirty, sinful, and an act of subjugation of the woman by the man. Great! For many thousands of years, you have thus overlooked what a wonderful instrument for liberation and independence, what a wonderful remedy for most diseases sex and love can be.

Most importantly: you have completely lost sight of the fact that, in the domain of sexual activity, absolutely everything is permitted, normal and healthy – if all participants involved are legally of age and fully assenting, without reservations and ulterior motives. Absolutely independently of whether they are married or not.

Most people have deep-rooted thinking habits; therefore it is difficult for them to change. But if you make your mind flexible by exercising self-discipline, you can easily change. The mind must be like play dough. Wisdom keeps the mind malleable. That is freedom. I wish that all mankind could experience this freedom from habits. Once you have freed yourself from the slavery of habits, you will know that there is no greater happiness than being a free child of Buddy´s and acting accordingly. (Yogananda)

With your twisted attitude you have transformed physical love into an instrument of power, traded goods, and an ego-booster. Ingenious. It's like someone who is sick pouring his healing herbal tea down the sink and eating the tea glass instead. As I've already mentioned: in some things you are even better than me!

I still remember all too well the anxiety I felt during my first experiences in this field, and especially my peers' primitive discussions about it. Tenderness meant being labelled a sissy. I found it repulsive but didn't know how to deal with it. Anyway, the separation of church and state was a great leap forward …

Right, you have introduced this separation many times, but primarily because of the lust for power of worldly tyrants and their wish not to be disturbed in their activities by the church tyrants. And look closely: despite the apparent separation of religion and politics, many of your secular laws reflect the destructive power of religions, especially when it comes to regulating love, marriage and sex, but also when it comes to "obedience to authority". Nowadays, hardly any elderly gentleman can sit alone near a playground and enjoy the sight of the unbridled vitality of children without being suspected of being a child molester. And then there is marriage. Some of them are actually made in "heaven", in our real home that is. But your vendors of religion have no access to this knowledge, otherwise they would

not have married so many couples that would have received *my* blessing instead!
And when it comes to divorce, you have put the religionists in charge. Because for not a second would Buddy think of standing in the way of two people divorcing if their marriage had become a toxic mess of mutual exploitation, lovelessness, negligence, etc. Better yesterday than tomorrow, that's what Buddy would say!
And just why would Buddy heartily approve of the "separation"? Because one cannot separate what was not joined, what didn´t belong together in true love in the first place. The external separation only reveals the *inner reality* of this relationship. Almost everywhere on earth you are still searching for the "guilty party" to legally dissolve what doesn't even exist. I couldn't have planned it any better!

Many people think it's better to stay together "for the sake of the children". However children are not stupid and sense what's going on anyway. Many would breathe a sigh of relief if the chronic conflicts came to an end.

You're right about that! Parents can't hide even the most camouflaged emotions from their children – still less from younger children! Children feel and see through every lie, and they are especially clear-sighted when it comes to the harmony between parents.

"Staying together for the sake of the kids" is an effective recipe for sad, stressful family life. *All* your thoughts influence family life – towards a sad uniform gray or towards a colorful, happy rainbow. And this applies everywhere, not just in the family but also at work.

I'll have to take a closer look at this question of the children of divorced parents.

Good, and then take an even *closer* look at the real children of divorced parents, by which you mean children with lasting emotional problems, don't you? The problems usually don't start to develop until *after* the divorce, when the parents start custody battles, or when one or both of them desperately want to prove that they were not to blame for the divorce.

Well, I've noticed this myself. Children are always under stress during a divorce, but not nearly so much if the parents maintain an amicable relationship afterwards, and especially if they make sure the children have no reason to feel that they might be responsible for the split. Ok, so how did you manage to channel the natural power of sex into dark realms?

As I've already told you, you managed to do that quite well without my help. One of your most successful methods of pushing love and sex into the swamps of the "dirty" was to twist, deliberately mistranslate or censor the words and actions of Buddy´s ambassadors. For example, you introduced the idea that people are "innocent" before they first experience physical love. This way of thinking is ingenious: the first time they have sex they lose their "innocence". So what are they afterwards? "Guilty"? Guilty of what? That they have become even more alive and cheerful?

True religion means unconditional love in the first place, love in the second place, and love in the third place. It does not stop at a happy, fulfilled sex life without rules, regulations, taboos, etc. Quite the opposite. Physical love, as Buddy has bestowed it on you people, is an expression of true religiosity! My representatives in the small, big and very large sects have done a great job. You have successfully attached the labels "savages" and "pagans" to primitive peoples who were light years ahead of you in this area, and deemed them "worthy of fighting against". Can you guess who the true primitives are here?

I need a short break now …

All right, you're doing really well so far. Have another espresso …

While the espresso shocks my palate, my mind reels. In one second, ten thousand questions are on the tip of my tongue, in the next there is complete emptiness. No matter how the evening turns out, I certainly won't forget it.

Ready for more? Did you want to ask a question?

Fortunately, my recording device is patient, and the battery is full. When it comes to sex, many religions attempt to convince us that contraception is a sin, and that you should only have sex to beget children because that's how Buddy created us.

Freedom is not achieved
by striving for freedom
but by striving for truth.
Freedom is not a goal
but a consequence.
Whenever you feel unfree,
seek the cause within yourself.
(Leo Tolstoi)

Ingenious, right? This came directly from me because I wanted to block this channel to Buddy too. Only a few of your wise men have reminded you, as an antidote to me, that free will and intelligence are also Buddy's gift. Intelligence that helps you to use natural contraception. So where is the problem? But I could use these twisted convictions about "sex only if you want to have children" quite well, because there's nothing like poverty and overpopulation to distract from Buddy and help to make people receptive to radical ideas.

Wow, yet another subject where ancient prejudices and taboos are so deeply ingrained that even talking about them is dangerous! What would be an effective devil hack for the individual in this case?

Hm, how about this? **Never compare yourself with other people and their sexual habits, let alone with their physical measurements and characteristics. Never take any notice of whatever kind of attempted interference ! And take to your heels at once if your partner in any way shows that you are not "good enough compared to what is normal or to what former partners did," etc. Especially when you are being made fun of! And the question "Darling, how was I?" has no place in love the way Buddy intended it for us. And never reveal your personal style of sexuality. Protect your double life.**

Could have a liberating effect, these words.

When two of you, regardless of gender, have reached the moment when a physical union would shine even more light on your relationship, there should be only two questions left to answer:
May our union be, first of all, an invitation to open the way to earth for a soul, and to accompany it for a few years as parents? If not, Buddy has given you enough intelligence not to extend this invitation. You call this "contraception".
And secondly: is what is happening complete, total, wholeheartedly and without reserve an expression of true togetherness, that is, "consensual"? If so, then there is nothing and no one who has a right to interfere – not with comment, comparison, directive, prohibition, disapproval, aversion, whatever.
Now this is crucial: as I've succeeded in wrapping physical love almost all over the world in a black fog of intolerance, fear and perversion, it is, as I said, absolutely necessary to lead a double life when you've become receptive to the light of truth. Meaning: your awakening to the genuine, real, beautiful and natural must not be clearly visible to the outside world but only ever in relation to the level of comprehension of those around you. Howl with the wolves, bleat with the sheep.

So no going "topless" on the beach when everyone else is wearing a bikini …

That would be an obvious example. And vice versa, I might add. Wearing a bikini on a nudist beach can cause trouble. My friend, real change always happens from within. The devil hack on the subject of sex, I would like to emphasize, applies exclusively to those “legally of age”.

But what about the physical turmoil prior to that, in puberty, when the hormones are dancing the tango? I was already everlastingly in love when I was six years old and a first-grader in elementary school, and at the age of ten I already had thoughts and dreams for which any priest would have condemned me to hell, had I confessed them. And I know for sure that almost every boy and every girl feels this way. It's just that they all remain alone with it, overwhelmed with chaotic feelings, and above all, with a bad conscience.

I'm sorry, you humans have such a twisted and disturbed relationship to sex, physical touch and tenderness! Anything I would truthfully have to say about a healthy physicality prior to reaching the age of consent would lead to you being blacklisted, or worse, after this conversation is published.
This much may be said: the mental and spiritual damage you take along with you from childhood and youth into adulthood in terms of sexuality is almost exclusively established by artificial moral concepts, not by the

emotional states endowed by Buddy on infants. The joy of living in your own body and enjoying the body of your friend, you earthlings turn into something "bad", "evil" *at any age*! And, as the height of folly, you do that primarily at the time when boys and girls naturally embark on a journey of discovery in the first place. *That* is a true crime against humanity which I did not intend to happen. Want a comparison? Imagine cutting out children's tongues and then expecting them to speak multiple languages from their eighteenth birthday onwards.

I think that's a bit extreme...

Not at all, my friend. It's even worse, but you can't fathom it because you're still missing a bit of tongue too. The good news is that the comparison is wrong! This "tongue" can grow back if you *will* it and allow it to, and you could free yourselves from the morality that poisoned your childhood and youth. It is possible and it is worth it.

Man, I could have used this devil back a long time ago. But what the heck, disappointments like this are part of life, right? At any rate, I'm sure it will save many readers from a fair bit of unhappiness.

If that's what they decide.

Yes, right. I'm glad you don't talk much about underage sex. There is so much wrong here, artificial and twisted, that I wouldn't know where to begin to heal the situation. What I do know for sure is that wherever physical touch and tenderness are prohibited, violence erupts. That reminds me: wherever sex is a taboo subject there are far more teenage pregnancies.

Exactly; where darkness reigns, people bash their heads against a brick wall more frequently. But in this case the light bringers are branded criminals. Here's a suggestion: replace the word "sex" with the words tender touch, caress, hug. These are as vital for the physical and mental-spiritual development of newborns, babies, toddlers, teenagers, adults and seniors as light, air, food and water! Wherever it is lacking, impoverishment, crippling, numbing, sexual addiction, dullness, controllability, despair, violence, lethargy, unpredictability, lack of self-confidence, apathy are the consequences … Sorry, but *this* list is virtually endless.
Now take a moment to consider who has an interest in awakening and happy vitality and independence – and who has an interest in numbing people down and making them dependent. I leave you with this brief but crucial information because I helped to bring about the situation, but now you have to heal it.

I'll do my best. One more delicate topic perhaps: What is your position on abortion? Fundamentalist Christians …

… are an abuse of the word "fundamentalist".

Excuse me?

Only a genuine Christian is a true fundamentalist Christian and should be permitted to call himself that. Violence, exclusion and racism would never be an option for him, only love. What you call "a fundamentalist" is in reality deluded fanaticism – it has as much to do with real religion as the glass splinter of an empty bottle of vodka in the gutter with the diamond in Queen Elizabeth's crown. Flimsy comparison, but you know what I mean.

Okay, I entirely agree with you, but I'm also aware that abortion is a very sensitive issue, and a fitting crusade for religious fanatics.

It is a delicate subject indeed, for me as well, because there is no real solution here, except on an individual level. I very rarely interfere here, although the fanatical fight against abortion naturally plays into my hands. Fanaticism and blindness always do. Here's some information to help with your decision: before birth, the soul itself chooses the body and the family for the next round and, as I've said, also its special task. Prior to birth, Buddy and her fellows "at home" are only available as benevolent advisers for the next steps and tasks …

Where are you?
You have spoken many words,
that others have put in your mouth.
Have you already said your own words? You have seen many things, that others pointed out to you.
Have you already looked with your own eyes?
You have done many things that others do.
Have you already let your heart act? You have felt a lot, when others say, that's how one feels.
Have you ever felt for yourself?
(Kerstin Allert Wybranietz)

Well, that reminds me of one of my darkest hours as a teenager. At that time I'd sunk into a deep depression because I couldn't stand the chronic tensions in my family any more, and of course saw myself as a victim, and sank into self-pity. Suddenly the thought came from out of the blue: "I'll pretend from now on that I chose these parents and this situation." What followed was like an enlightenment and on that basis I succeeded in pulling myself out of the swamp. So you're telling me I did actually choose my parents myself?

Without a doubt. And that goes for each time you return to earth. You could save yourself many problems if you realized that it is your choice whether you are white or black, yellow or red this time. Yes, even whether you will be a man or woman. But that is not important now. Just take this information at face value for now, and think about it later.

Well, I'm not asking for a recommendation on the subject, just for your view of things. I think many readers could benefit from this advice.
A question on the subject of children at this point: and I have a personal interest when I ask about a problem or make an observation. We've already broached this topic: how is it that so many parents make the same mistakes with their children as they suffered from as children in their own families? This happens all over the world and in all social classes.

This all works together in my favor. From Nero, Caligula, Alexander, Duterte, Maduro, Mugabe, Castro to Stalin, Mussolini, Kim Yong Un, Orban, Erdogan, Genghis Khan, Mao, Pol Pot, Pinochet, Franco, Amin, Duvalier, Netanyahu, and various popes up to Hitler, Putin, Trump, Bolsonaro, yes, to the block leader and mini tyrant around the corner from you, to the neighbor who won't let you live in peace. Almost all cold tyrants, whether great or small, are weak people who were too cowardly to assign the oppression and unkindness of their childhood years to the originators and thereby absolve themselves. They are unconsciously in permanent revenge mode and only trust other tyrants, if anyone at all. Hence the good relations within the Thimble Gang.

"Thimble gang"? Did I hear you right?

That's what we call the tyrants of the world, or rather their apprentices, aspirants, followers and imitators. As it's not a short list, so that I don't have to keep repeating myself let's refer to them this way from now on.

How did the name come about?

Quite simply, before birth these souls have chosen a life that hands them a thimbleful of power – for wise use or thoughtless abuse, that is always left to free will. They cultivate good relations with one another because they see in each other a justification for their own way and admire each other for it – and thus themselves. Hence the origin of your proverb that "there is honor among thieves".

Yes, they are even grateful for the existence of other despots, because each of them has a conscience, even if only on the smallest scale. After they've whitewashed themselves as "good" and their own actions as "justified", it's only a small step to treating their children in the same way. In this way, the perpetrator experiences another perverse form of justification of his actions.

Okay, could you explain to me in more detail your role with the monsters of the "thimble gang"? Did you "make" them all? If so, you would definitely terrify me!

From giving comes wealth,
from discipline comes happiness,
patience results in attractive forms,
endeavor results in the fulfilment of wishes, from concentration comes peace, and from wisdom comes freedom from impediments. (Nagarjuna)

No, don't worry. The devil is not evil, he is just no good as a tour guide in your life! But this is a delicate subject, and the truth will certainly not please many of your readers. Really you'll derive more benefit from getting to the heart of this yourself so as to learn how to prevent the catastrophes caused by such people. It's really important to tackle the actions of these monsters in society. Sweeping them under the carpet just guarantees that it will happen again in the future. And I do mean tackle, not revenge.

That sounds inadequate to me …

Alright, just this much: Hitler is not Hitler, just as Trump isn´t Trump, or the house tyrant in your neighborhood, or the hated teacher, and so on. All these people … hang on a minute … do you know the saying: "What if there's a war, and nobody shows up?"

Of course, I once threw it at my father when he mocked me because I wanted to become a "conscientious objector".

And now think what would have happened if more than half of the Germans hadn't voted for Hitler. Or millions of Americans for Trump. Or if nobody had listened to Nero, Stalin and all the other monsters.

I think I know what you're getting at. These people only have so much power because it was given to them by us.

The thimble gang, in a sense, are empty shells without a life of their own. They have wrapped their souls up in a thick layer of mental concrete. Their actions are the echo of millions of followers and their craving for the fulfilment of promises. They are longing to plug the holes in their souls. Holes pierced by a childhood and an adolescence that tempted them to neglect free will and compassion and let them dry up. Every single one of those people who raise tyrants onto their pedestals has the opportunity to say "no" and to peel off the pent-up anger and pain and dissolve it into thin air. With each day passing that they fail to do so, their shame and false pride, which make changing course seem impossible, will grow.

The gold miner's problem again.

Right. And even that is just imaginary: anyone can, at any time, return to Buddy and would find the door open. You wouldn't even have to knock, the door is always open. But you don't go through it because the feelings of guilt under the carpet block self-forgiveness. My role in all this? I pointed in the wrong direction, I led into temptation, I whispered: "You must follow orders, not think and not feel."
But I want you and all your readers to understand that I do not actively *direct* anyone's steps, I do not carry anyone into the darkness. No one in the whole universe is permitted to infringe on and tamper with free will. Whoever manages to fully develop free will in their lives are free people, even behind prison walls. And they are never surprised when they reap what they have sown, for better or worse.

I understand … But how long it will take me to digest this, I don't know. Just to distract myself a little: the example of not knocking on the children's room door that we discussed earlier is still on my mind …

Yes, let's repeat: the numbing and distracting from the right path begins on the very first day of life, as I've said before; I was there at that very moment. And as I've already indicated: all over the world, parents determine the lives of their children to an extent that is completely inexplicable. No gardener runs out at night to his plants, tears them up just to see if they have taken root! And no gardener sows the good seed, then turns around and only returns when the veggies are already rotten. But that's what you do for eighteen years with your children, and you don't give over until you can be certain that it was successful, the confusion and tangle of ignoring, drilling, shaping, molding and kneading in your own image. And often, even then, there's no end to the meddling, thanks to some chronic worry that you burden your children with, and which pursues them into adulthood. And if a "black sheep" has managed to escape and go its own way, you'll blame yourself for the rest of your life because the child has "turned out badly".

That all sounds very familiar to me when I look around my circle of friends.

Yes, "black sheep" is a label often applied to those who walk their own path in life, just as Buddy intended for this little sheep. As for entering the children's room without knocking: just think some more about this profound and ongoing violation of human dignity, and what this triggers in the everyday life of the family, and the injury it causes. How can the child escape from such "normality" without breaking with the people it actually wants to love, on whose goodwill it depends? Breaking with them would be the more courageous, healthier decision, because by repressing it all, the child breaks *twice* – with the parents and with itself.

As I said, and as you'd already recognized yourself: the main reason why mental and spiritual injuries caused by the "traditions of parental abuse" do not return to the sender later in life but are inflicted on their own children or other people in their private or professional life, is hidden in this and other similar contexts.

And it´s done in full self-righteousness. The act of giving it back to the parents would in fact be tantamount to admitting that one was timid back then. It erodes your self-esteem and creates shame that you put up with the humiliation for so long. "I was beaten as a child, and it hasn't done me any harm." Sounds familiar?

Do not constantly think about everything you've done wrong. Forget it, because concentrated attention evokes habits and memories.

As soon as the needle sinks onto a record, the record starts to play. Attention is like a needle playing the record of past actions. You should therefore not focus your attention on bad actions. Why do you still want to suffer because of past foolishness? Banish them from your mind and just be careful not to repeat such actions. True repentance means turnaround and a new beginning, not self-accusation and a guilty conscience. (Yogananda)

But of course! A classmate from school recently uttered it at a class reunion after thirty years. He didn't have the slightest awareness of how much it had hurt him – after three marriages and four children who don't want to have any contact with him.

So why do so many parents enter their children's room at any time of day or night, without knocking, absolutely convinced of their right to do so? Because unconditional love and genuine trust are such a rare combination worldwide. Children are often seen as an investment that's supposed to pay off. The links in the endless chain that slowly constricts their body and mind start with activities as infants and toddlers, when "something must be achieved" nonstop. They glide over endless days and nights in school and high school, where homework is so extensive that the children often sit in front of the books at midnight, pumped full of coffee or harder drugs to keep themselves awake, and end up, at the least, with student loans that can only be paid back with the greatest of difficulty and hardship over the course of decades. If they have not fallen into private bankruptcy by then.

Mamma mia, exactly! And when I rattled the chains and made it clear to the teachers what I thought of them, because I couldn't stand all this insanity of normality any more, I got into trouble with my parents, and they marched to the school to apologize for me. "The Insanity of Normality" – that's the title of a book, by the way, I can highly recommend it. Arno Gruen is the author's name.

I remember, the man tries to shine some light into your cellar. Yes, at every stage of your life's journey, my strategy was to ensure that the next link in the chains of the future slave, his enslavement perfect because unconscious, would glisten in bright, attractive colors – and would also promise the fulfilment of his life´s dream, if not today, then tomorrow at the latest.

Note that the promises almost always refer to something material, enumerable, comparable with something else. To summarize, "Money makes you happy." "Greed is good." "Power is what it's all about." The goal is the greener grass on the other side of the fence, the bigger third car, the more colorful garden gnome, the more beautiful wife, the trophy husband. Many of you fall into my traps and consider people who are loaded with wealth to be "better", "blessed" by Buddy. Nothing could be further from the truth, and the fact that the suicide rate among millionaires is higher

than in any other cohort should give you pause for thought.

I've had my own experience with that ...

Material wealth of any kind is nothing but a test, namely of how humanely and generously you deal with the energy that is put into your hands. Because "money" is nothing but a form of energy, similar to electricity.
And so the fear will always accompany you: if social security, employment protection, maternity provision, etc. have been left out in the struggle to acquire money, then you live in constant fear and danger of being fired. Petty errors, a misstep, a lapse, a whim, the wrong clothes – and you're out on the street, often literally. Most companies today are small tyrannies with tight hierarchies, even many startups by young people. These, my friend, are the famous "Western values" that you defend and justify with so much dedication. A successful recipe for the destruction of your basic needs and livelihoods.

My head is throbbing ... I realize just how easy it would be to evade your temptations ...

The purpose and value of a goal are in the eye of the beholder.

How true …

Every region of our planet holds energy that can be harnessed with the help of the true blessings of technology and science.
Where there is little wind, there is a lot of sun. Where there is little sun, there is a lot of water. Where there is no water, there is much geothermal energy. Where one form of energy is too little, another one is there in abundance.
A "peaceful" nuclear reactor, on the other hand, is nothing less than a "peaceful" atomic bomb. Nuclear power as a source of energy is a technology that cannot be controlled for all of the future – a dead end. "All is lost if we are determined not to give up anything."
(The Translator)

Your materially oriented value system has yet another intrinsic problem, because you have let yourselves be trained and drilled to the conviction that only someone with a job has any worth. Well, in Buddy's eyes, of course, this is utter nonsense – think of the parable of the lilies in the field. But this baseless belief is very persistent. After all, it's like this: almost all of your ostensible progress is aimed at abolishing labor in almost every form. But so far you have completely overlooked the fact that work is gradually evolving from duty and necessity to privilege.

Hey! That's always been my feeling! My parents and grandparents back then lived to work, but we're supposed to work to live!

Your economic power today would be sufficient to let everyone between the ages of eighteen and fifty-five work only twenty hours a week, to pay a decent living wage with money to save, to pay *everyone* a basic income above the poverty threshold, to feed a world population exclusively with organic food. AND to pay every person a pension from the age of fifty-five onward, enough to live well on.
On top of that, you could provide water, electricity, internet and public transport, completely clean and environmentally neutral and *free of charge,* for everyone in the world. All the material prerequisites for that are already there.

Man, that's right, but nobody dares to think like that. No, that's not true, there are futurologists who've shown us the way. The Club of Rome, for example ...

Right, many of you know that very well. If military spending worldwide were reduced by a quarter – all that would be possible right away. A man among you called Walter Rathenau had this to say, a hundred years ago:

"What should we shed tears about? About politics? About the people? One month of war costs could eliminate all misery. Another month could protect all spiritual people for eternity. A third month could make a paradise of the cities. A fourth month could liberate research, a fifth could liberate art from every material bond and fetter."

Time and again, you have successfully dismissed people with common sense as naïve "utopians" just because they realized you could turn this planet into an absolute paradise at any time. I'm the realist here. That's why I was so successful a seducer. I know exactly where to start. Want an example? I presented as a fact the illusion that land ownership is associated with neither duty nor any responsibility to treat this piece of living earth and its creatures with care and wisdom. You then gradually transformed land ownership into something sacred which gives the owner the absolute power of a slave owner over the land. Disputes over land ownership and border fences are among your favorite hobbies.

That can't be denied. But to ask it the other way around: why are you, all of a sudden, an expert on what would turn the world into a paradise?

All of a sudden? Well, my friend, if it is my task to seduce you into error and lead you astray, then I can only succeed if I know your actual destiny, right? I can

lead you onto crooked paths only when I know exactly where the straight and narrow path is.
By the way, here's a question: why do you think a lack of money in government agencies almost always leads to spending cuts in the funding of art and culture first?

Logically, because these are considered to be the least important things in everyday life.

No, on the contrary. Because almost every form of art and culture conceals strong threats to those in power and to large corporations. The real satisfaction that could be gained as a gift in the practice of art makes you independent, especially independent from the compulsion to consume. And it is always intellectual and spiritual independence that tyrants fear most. Drugs are bought only by those who are addicted.

And large corporations fear nothing more than frugality and contentment…

Right. Friends, it would be possible for you to create a paradise, in next to no time; however, you opt for the way of the ego, greed and fear. You also 'democratically' vote for those fools who lead you into the abyss – and then you're surprised when the sea level rises and floods many of your cities.

You make your workers and the middle class pay much higher taxes than those for capital gains, interest, etc. That means you exploit workers and reward lottery players. Ideal conditions for the next civil war.

Yes, so many things are topsy-turvy.

One of the happiest days of mankind will be when manual labor is no longer automatically considered "lesser" than intellectual labor. Good and cheerful bakers, dedicated organic farmers, loving nurses do far more for the progress of mankind than academics who do not love life. It's completely wrong to base income on the length of education. True intelligence has nothing to do with rote learning, or being able to maneuver yourself into the dead end of expertise. Head in the sand, that is your strategy. Almost every child has more heart and brain than your politicians. Look at Greta Thunberg. She's one of those people who might yet save you from yourselves.

I will really do my best. Now a question comes to mind, perhaps because I read an article about it on the flight: the Western world – or the entire world, come to that – is confronted with the problem of refugee avalanches, whether because of war, the climate or economic disaster in their own country. Did you have a hand in all this too? After all, this phenomenon threatens the imaginary security we've lulled ourselves into.

Good question, but put as if you couldn't even begin to imagine the actual causes. Am I right?

Well going by our conversation so far, then the migration problem worldwide is a consequence of conditions initiated by you and which humanity itself is equally responsible for, from exploitation and starvation in colonial times to climate refugees.

Floods of migrants are a consequence of your own actions. Sowing and reaping, you remember? To solve any problem, you must understand and eliminate the real causes, not just the symptoms. You are still far too convinced that it's enough just to suck away the smoke to extinguish a fire.

As well as an objective investigation into the causes, you need to look into two aspects of the refugee problem if you want to find lasting solutions. Anyone who believes that heartless populism is a key is an idiot on the wrong track.

Point one: refugees do not come just like that, they would gladly stay and help improve their homeland and solve their own problems. But in the many centuries of economic exploitation and the colonial policies of "the master race", of selfish monetary policy and completely misapplied "development aid", you have fostered the conditions in the countries of the second and third world that triggered the refugee flows in the first place.

A famine somewhere? You supply industrial wheat, milk powder and sugar so that the population becomes tired and dependent. The burning of fossil fuels and your meat-based diet are partly responsible for climate change and thus for the climate flight. You have sown the wind and harvested the storm!
Point two: so you have caused the flight yourself. Now what? What about the integration of refugees? You have to realize that successful integration is absolutely necessary, and that it should not be overlooked out of misguided respect for certain customs and traditions of the refugees …

But they also bring many interesting and beneficial things with them which we can learn from! Starting with their skills in cooking and traditional craftsmanship. In any case, I've found many aspects of their cultures fascinating during my travels.

Good point, but that's not what I mean. You have to teach the immigrants certain rules under which you live and make sure that they are followed. But you often don't have the courage to do this because it is "politically incorrect". But if you allow refugees to rebuild, in your country, destructive aspects of cultural coexistence in their home countries, then they will create the same conditions in *your* country that were aspects of their reasons for fleeing. Examples? Corruption, roles for women and children, authoritarian hierarchies, macho culture, religious fanaticism, a destructive concept of "honor", intolerance. Wherever such conditions prevail, division, poverty – and flight – always arise. The devil hack here: **education, education, education! Acknowledging these facts, showing real remorse, asking for forgiveness, ending the exploitation and extending genuine aid, all that could be assistance for self-help.**

Man is part of the whole that we call the universe, a part limited in space and time. He experiences himself, his thoughts and feelings, as separate from everything else – a kind of optical illusion of consciousness. This illusion is like a prison for us which limits us to our own preferences and to affection for just a few.

Our goal must be to free ourselves from this prison by expanding the horizon of our compassion until it encompasses all living beings and all of nature in all its beauty. (Albert Einstein)

It makes me want to tear my hair out in frustration! Why do we calves choose our butchers ourselves, why don't we see that the thimble gang will never act for our benefit?

As I've already said: because you elect not people but the promises they symbolize and serve you piecemeal. And because you do not trust your knowledge of human nature, your intuition. You elect feelings – namely hope and artificially inflated self-esteem. Hitler was elected because German parents raised generations of obedient cowards who happily followed the "strong man" who promised to make up for their lack of self-confidence. The members of the thimble gang … We've already talked about them: essentially, they are mere puppets, without any self-awareness, in my extensive servant entourage. They are all schoolroom bullies at the level of fourteen-year-olds who would step over dead bodies just to preserve their own self-image. And they work hard at concealing the fears and inner emptiness that drive them. Where others have their human dignity as well as their basic trust and self-confidence, they have a large black hole clamoring to be filled with recognition, applause, and unconditional submissiveness. These people no longer expect love because they would not recognize it, even if it hit them right between the eyes. They are insatiable – and that is a characteristic unknown to love.

That's been my observation as well.

These tyrannical robots are the mouthpiece for all those who are always looking for others to blame for their own misery. Fearful people elect them because they promise to take away their fear without having to find out where the fear comes from. Rich people elect them because they promise to dispel the unconscious feeling of meaninglessness in their lives, and to help them become even richer. Poor people elect them because they promise to create jobs, even though they could find them more easily on their own, and because they promise to repair their damaged self-esteem. People in general elect them for confirmation that global warming

isn't real, that oil and coal will be available indefinitely, and that Buddy made mistakes when she created the black, red and yellow races.

They elect them like termites elect a top termite that promises that the wooden house they are about to eat up will provide food and shelter forever and ever. Reasonable people who murmur that "growth at all costs won't work" are ignored, blocked, fired, locked up, pilloried. Tried and tested practice.

Global warming? That's presented as a fairy tale, invented by the Greens to deprive people of their third car!

Truly, if you don't manage the transition from progress by means of growth to conservation, you'll be just like the termites that eat up the wooden house – convinced that it "will last forever".

Now that's plausible, I can sense the truth of it. In the past, I used to admire a braggart because, unlike me, he seemed to have courage. Until one day I read why criminals serving a life sentence sometimes find women outside prison who want to marry them. If you asked the women, they almost always said: "At least he had guts." Oh dear!

And as for the rich who still think that material possessions are the key to happiness: I once wanted to write a book about people who won millions in the lottery. What they felt at the beginning, how life had changed after four weeks – and how they lived five years later. I dropped the plan very quickly – it would have been a very sad book, of no use to anyone.

I remember, I talked you into writing the book anyway because, back then, I preferred to see you being deeply depressed. I put on the brakes wherever I could …

Gee, you really had my best interests at heart. It actually took me some time to say goodbye to this idea … Another topic comes to my mind, one close to my heart: what role does sport play in your plan as a brakeman? Because sport hasn't existed as a mass phenomenon for all that long. Another one of your inventions as well? For me, sport was life-saving in a way because I was able to "rebuild" the ruins of my self-confidence.

It took me quite a while to subdue and dominate sport because originally the basic idea came from friends of Buddy´s on the other side of the playing field. Sport was supposed to help find a sort of outlet for those emotions that formerly used to lead straight to warmongering. In the beginning, it worked out well, especially because in England "fair play", the "fair match" and unconditional respect for the opponent were held up high. But then I came up with a double strategy to turn the tide in my favor. First, I put money into the game. An almost infallible recipe.

A hundred million dollars for a football player …

As the hand held in front of the eye covers the largest mountain, so the small earthly life covers the view, the immense lights and mysteries which the world is full of, and whoever can pull it off the eyes, like one pulls away a hand, that one beholds the great glow in the inner world. (Martin Buber)

With the consequence that you almost exclusively worship the winners in sports – and, at the same time, you are deaf and blind to the fact that the winner owes his prize money, medals and trophies to only one circumstance, namely that there is a loser! Every winner should kiss the feet of the second, third, fourth and last! No one would stand on the winner's podium if they were not surrounded by non-winners. Today, only a few places also respect the silver and bronze medal winners, although they are as indispensable to the winners as the roots of a tree are to its crown. How impoverished are the thoughts and feelings of a person who ignores or sneers at the roots of a tree and reveres the crown only! There are no schools and very few parents drawing attention to this state of affairs, making genuine cooperation possible. Yes, I had many tools of silence and ignorance at my disposal.

And the second restraint on sport?

You have three guesses! Laziness, of course. And competitive thinking. I managed to constrain children's natural urge to move, their joy in letting off steam, in dancing and getting to know their bodies and their limits – in gym class, through over-protective parents who drive their children to school, and so on and so forth. Every child whose individual mobility and agility is criticized in the name of standardized practices finds his enthusiasm stifled. Finally many of you turn into fat couch potatoes, until you almost all say: "No thanks, I can't dance." Crazy, because everyone can dance – if there is no one around to laugh at him.

The lack of exuberant exercise which is prevalent almost everywhere in the Western world has a side effect that I wanted and programmed. Do you know what I'm talking about?

Hmmm, I can only tell you about my own experience: I used to be very athletic and able to teach my body pretty much anything, from handstands and somersaults to playing handball and engaging in martial arts. This made me better at estimating energy flows in everyday life, for example when driving a car, in physics class, when visualizing material processes, etc. When doing repairs and handicraft work, for example, I could work out how things were connected. I was able to assemble Ikea cabinets without any instructions. I also believe that an athletic architect has a better feel for materials and statics. People who have problems with mobility, whose natural love of movement has been suppressed, have much bigger problems with the flow of energies, well into adulthood.

That's what I meant. If you don't know the limits of your own body and don't want to play and dance, you are actually much easier to control. You lose courage, also mentally, because you are not able to evaluate and adapt to energy flows in any given situation. He can't "read the air," as the Japanese say. In general you cannot develop a good sense of balance, literally and in your mind.

That's exactly my experience. By the way: what about the oriental martial arts that have a spiritual element? I've always had the feeling that they represent something special, particularly Aikido and Tai Chi.

That's right, but only very few teachers still take this original element into account; almost everywhere it is primarily about inflating the ego, at best about health and fitness and self-defense. To quote Ed Parker, one of the greatest karate teachers, who was almost immune to my tricks: "***Insecurity is the only reason why people fight; someone has to prove that he is better or stronger than someone else. A person who is***

sure of himself does not have to prove anything by force, so he can leave a fight with dignity and pride. He is the true martial artist – a man so strong inside that he has no need to demonstrate his strength. The key point in mastering martial arts is the ability to avoid physical confrontation rather than winning it. It is this attitude of inner certainty that is conveyed to the opponent - he will realize that he cannot win, even if he wins."

Hmm, I sometimes enjoy watching sports on TV and feel good whenever I can do something for my body by cycling and swimming. But what the heck, I don't have to let you spoil my fun.

Way to go.

This reminds me of an anecdote told by Giorgio Sapia, my first Aikido teacher. One day a prospective student asked him: "How long will it take you to make me invincible?" Giorgio looked at the clock and said: "Twelve hours". "Super! But that's hard to believe!", said the newcomer. "Twelve hours, then the stores will open and I'll buy you a gun." He was a good teacher, I'm very grateful to him … Speaking of fun: the biggest spoilsports in the world today are terrorists all of all colors and origins. But you're all in on this, aren't you?

No, only indirectly in this case as well. Remember my words: "A small child can uproot a tiny weed. Give it time and you won't be able to pull it out with a crane." I have sown a tiny seed, and centuries later it has become a weed called terrorism. Can you imagine what this seed was like back then? Don't forget that almost all terrorist leaders came from wealthy families.

Saving the planet
is not a spectator sport.
(Lester R. Brown)

If you look at terrorism on a very small scale, namely within families and in the schoolyard, then I would say its origin is the inability of parents to treat their children with genuine kindness. Fathers don't show emotions and talk about wanting to "toughen up" their sons in order to turn personal inadequacy and emotional coldness into something seemingly positive. And the mothers participate in this form of "upbringing" by supporting the fathers or by not protecting their sons or daughters from such fathers, so betraying the children.

Exactly, you're getting close. The fact that men don't want to show feelings, that they have learned to see them as a sign of "weakness", is at the root of many problems today. Essentially, a terrorist is a person who cannot or will not feel empathy, almost always because he was forced in early childhood to somehow numb and subdue his own pain. But the fact is: *You cannot numb feelings selectively!* You cannot tell yourself: "I'll only suppress the negative feelings, and I'll nurture and care for all the positive ones." Imagine you want to sharpen your sense of smell so as to become the best spice dealer, but you want to kill off the same sense so that you won't notice your girlfriend´s bad breath. That's impossible, benumbed is benumbed. This is one of the main reasons why the world has a drug problem.

I can see that. By the way: what other reasons are there for the drug epidemic?

Various causes, but also because you have learned nothing from the various attempts at prohibition. Prohibiting alcohol makes it all the more enticing. Alternatively, you could teach your kids how to handle it responsibly. It is the same with drugs. Do you know why politicians have long been opposed to decriminalizing cannabis, marijuana and hashish?

Because they are thought to be gateways to harder, more destructive drugs.

That is a lie. They have been hiding behind this fig leaf. Alcohol is many times more destructive, as you can see from any statistic about it. The fact is, those who consume these "soft" drugs become a little more relaxed and laidback in everyday life. They are no longer easy prey for consumerist frenzies, consequently sales decline in all areas of industrial production. This is already being felt by all states that have approved the use of these drugs. But they cannot go back. The bottom line is that drugs are a bit like pillows that are supposed to soften the harshness of everyday life. They wouldn't be necessary if … But you have to figure that out for yourself.

Okay, on the subject of mind-altering drugs such as LSD, psilocybin and the like, a master from Afghanistan once related an allegory. He said that these drugs "are like a ladder that you put on the walls of paradise. You climb up, take a look into the Garden of Eden, and you are so overwhelmed with the sights that you fall off the ladder and break a bone. The period of healing postpones the realization, attained through meditation and practice, that the wall exists only in the imagination." This little parable alone has kept me off of drugs of all kinds.

Yes, I know that man, he's always been a thorn in my side, and throwing spanners in the works …

Bad for you, good for me. Okay, back to terrorism in the world today: how can we get rid of it, after triggering it ourselves?

Copycats are everywhere – it's obviously an attractive job description.

The terrorists all over the world – in whatever political or religious guise – are successful, they are winning. But to this day you are hardly aware as to *why*! They have succeeded in their main goal, to instill chronic fear into the minds of many people, thanks to an unholy alliance of certain media that appeals to base instincts – under the guise of "the public's right to know". And this in spite of all experience and statistics that clearly prove that, today, it is safer to live almost anywhere on this planet than twenty or thirty years ago.
Secondly, the terrorists have succeeded in giving your politicians the justification for sweeping surveillance measures that put you under the ever-vigilant microscope of the "authorities". Democratic elections? A fig leaf ritual to give the little tyrants a pseudo-legitimacy. The mechanics of terrorism play so much into the hands of the authorities that no one would be surprised if it turned out that Al Qaeda and Isis were and are subdivisions of Western intelligence agencies.
Certainly no one would be surprised if they could still remember *who* the USA actually used to promote and still does in order to protect their interests all over the world. The fact is, you almost always reap what you have sown.

Greed and fear, powerful tools …

Which feeling creates the strongest dependency? Fear. How do I keep people fearful in order to enslave them? By stirring up fear whilst at the same time convincing them that I'm their savior. Throughout history churches, sects, cults and tyrants have used this method to mentally and physically enslave billions of people.
So what served my interests? Terrorism. If there is too little of it, it is promoted abroad through corruption, the import of weapons and ideology, until eventually it comes back to you.

And the media get involved because of click rates and sales figures.

My obedient servants! They report for weeks on end a terrorist attack with three deaths, but do they say a single word about the fifteen thousand children who die of hunger every day, or the hundreds of thousands who owe their death from heart failure to your food industry? Think about it: one thousandth of the money spent worldwide on fighting terrorism would be enough to eliminate all hunger in the world, and to deprive all the potential terrorists of one of the main justifications for their insane actions. What have you done with Buddy´s gifts, namely reason, foresight, intelligence and free will?

Man, I feel ashamed, and even more interested in how to end terrorism. Is there a reliable remedy? I'm guessing not — or is there?

A Chinese story tells of an old farmer who had only an old horse to help him work the fields. One day, the horse escaped into the mountains, and when all the neighbors regretted the farmer´s bad luck, he just replied: "Bad luck? Good luck? Who knows?" A week later, the horse returned from the mountains with a herd of wild horses, and this time the neighbors congratulated him for his luck. The farmer just said: "Bad luck? Good luck? Who knows?" When the farmer's son tried to tame one of the wild horses, the animal threw him off and he broke his leg. Everyone thought that was bad luck. But not the farmer, who said: "Bad luck? Good luck? Who knows?". A few weeks later, the military marched into the village and enlisted every able-bodied young man they could find. Everyone except the peasant boy. Good luck? Bad luck? Who knows? (Anthony de Mello)

You and your readers won't like the answer, because it is so simple that it seems naïve and impractical, especially given your veneration for the media and

"freedom of speech". Here is the ultimate devil hack, the solution:
You have to take away the public platform that terrorists can use. Turn off the spotlights. Do not report their crimes. Ignore them completely. Pretend they do not exist. That's exactly what would have to happen.

In fact this would be almost impossible, but I still feel it could work. On the other hand, I think that terrorists would then fight for even more publicity, wouldn't they?

But of course! Of course they would fight for some time, like little children in a sandbox, but it doesn't matter how angry they get. What makes you think that the deaths of thousands in traffic accidents, or tens of thousands of starving children, are less significant than the death of victims of terrorism? All of you have to stand up and spread the truth. You must tell people the truth, the real facts.

What are the real facts, for example in the case of Islamist terrorists?

This would also dispel some of your prejudices. Because the undeniable truth is that Islamist terrorists have as much to do with true Islam as the Inquisition has to do with the work of Jesus. True Islam is an absolutely humane religion. Hospitality, for example, is sacred to it. Take a bike ride from Morocco to the Philippines, it will open your eyes. You'll most likely have to spend hardly any money along the way.

My Afghan friend once told me that there is a saying in Islam: "If you do not allow me to extend my hospitality to you, you will make me a sinner." In fact, I've never experienced it any other way.

And by the way: Islam in no way orders women to wear veils or headscarves. This custom was copied from Byzantine Christians by self-appointed pushers of the Islamic religion.

I didn't know that, but I suspected it. A Muslim acquaintance told me that there's only one passage in the Quran concerned with women's clothing. It states they may "dress appropriately". Different clothing is appropriate on the beach in Hawaii than in the streets of Delhi or in an Istanbul mosque. It is up to each individual to decide. A question here: can you explain why I get such a strange feeling at the sight of a woman veiled except for a slit for her eyes – as if a threat permeates the air. I always feel uncomfortable, and usually I look away so that I don't have to analyze this feeling more closely.

That is understandable, and a sign of your intuitive development. You sense the many centuries of oppression and exploitation, of which the veiling is only a symbolic remnant. You have all overlooked something. Take a closer look at the arguments of the advocates of veiling, whether man or woman. The veiling allegedly serves as "protection". Protection from what? From the lascivious looks and thoughts of men? A rhetorical question for reflection: who protects unveiled men from the lascivious looks and thoughts of women? And secondly: has it never occurred to you that a woman turns into a sexual object when she wears a veil? Because the male observer wonders what paradisal sight might be concealed behind it. The veil is like a match on the firebomb of urges and desires, isn't it?

Oops, you've seen right through me — that's exactly what I've often felt at the sight of a veil. The sight of an unveiled woman rarely causes such feelings…

Thirdly, and even more importantly: isn't it a pathetic sign of impotence on the part of oh so weak-willed men if they cannot be expected to take responsibility for their thoughts and feelings? *This is the actual crime of veiling.* Because it clearly reinforces the conviction that men are naturally weak and unable to control themselves, that they are *naturally* slaves to their emotions when they see a beautiful woman that they desire. It amounts to a ban on men becoming adults. That, in turn, leads them to believe that they have a right to women who do not veil themselves but who display their Buddy-given beauty.

I hadn't looked at it from this angle before.

Perhaps because you're a man? But seriously, something even more harmful happens as a consequence – something overlooked by your psychological science: *all human beings have an indestructible and eternal soul from which they cannot hide their own inner truth.* Every self-deceiving man who refuses to take responsibility for his thoughts, feelings and actions, unconsciously acknowledges that he is *fundamentally* weak.

But he must hide this *real* weakness at all costs from himself and the world, from parents, peers and especially from women! This results in a rigid mask, an artificial pose of strength and self-confidence with all its ugly consequences, all the way up to the use of violence on both the small and large scale. It is a law of nature that whoever subjugates others can never have self-respect.

That explains it - it's an exact description of the root of my feeling! I sensed the centuries of violence on both sides behind the symptom! But don't forget, you wanted to elaborate further on how to stop Islamist terrorists in particular. What else should we know and circulate about Islam?

All Muslims as well as all Christians and all other people are equal. All are brothers and sisters. An imam, priest, pope or religious scholar is equal to every other person. He cannot order or instruct anyone what to do. This applies to any terrorist motive, because every use of violence – with only a few exceptions – is a sign of weakness and leads nowhere. This also applies to every wall constructed between states. Here's a special devil hack, a basic law:

A person who helps to strengthen the sense of "we" in a community of people, the feeling for togetherness, harmony and mutual support, is a good person.

A person who helps to strengthen the sense of togetherness, harmony and mutual support in a community of people, but who, at the same time, tries to convince the members that they are "better" than non-members – that person is a brainwasher, an enemy of the people. He has no credibility whatsoever.

It does not matter whether the "community of people" is a family or municipality, a city, an association, a party, a religion, a country, a state.

Our bodies are our gardens to the which our wills are gardeners. So that if we will plant nettles or sow lettuce, set hyssop and weed up thyme, supply it with one gender of herbs or distract it with many – either to have it sterile with idleness, or manured with industry – why, the power and corrigible authority of this lies in our wills.
(William Shakespeare, Othello)

That probably applies to most groups and organizations, because most people consider themselves to be something better than others – or at least something special, don't they?

Yep, with the consequences you can see in the news every day.

Even more food for thought here. Earlier you said that two things came to mind, firstly patriotism, and we've already talked about that, and secondly?

Ah yes, you're up for that now! I wanted to talk about one of my great feats, namely the veneration of the concept of "identity".

And what's wrong with that?

Nothing – if your identity serves as a springboard to ever *new* identities, to learning experiences, quantum leaps in development, to independence, freedom of thought and feeling.
Everything about it is wrong if your identity serves as a justification for stagnation, for "always doing things the traditional way", for contempt for otherness and thinking differently, for fear of the foreign, the new, for freezing by clinging to the past and routine.
As I said, every human being has a unique, distinctive soul that returns to this earth again and again – sometimes as a man, sometimes as a woman, sometimes as a black man, sometimes as a white woman, sometimes yellow, green, blue, sometimes with a silver spoon in his mouth, sometimes as a nomad, sometimes as the daughter of a prostitute, sometimes as the son of a count, sometimes as the daughter of a murderer, sometimes as the son of a baker. So what does "identity" mean? Do you now understand my goal with the establishment and veneration of personal identity?

Yet again my mind's buzzing with thoughts, but I'm starting to make out a theme in the confusion. So my true identity is not something I have to create first, right?

Ab-so-lute-ly right! But you've taken it to such an extreme that someone feels seriously threatened in his "identity" if the skull tattooed on his neck isn't considered to be super stylish. This does not mean that your unique and unmistakable being must not have any recognizable features – but you have made a quasi-religion out of it. If you have found the ideal person for a leading position, but his opponents can prove by means of forty-year-old home cinema snippets that he once picked his nose at the age of fourteen, then he is disqualified. My plan with the worship of identity worked perfectly here, unfortunately. You have turned your identity into an effective barrier to curiosity and learning. And you have concealed the fact that a person who made many mistakes in his youth and in his life, but *learned* from them, is much more suitable as a politician than a person with a "clean" past. But I think the topic of "identity" is quite comprehensible so that I don´t have to dwell on it any longer.

I agree.

Before I forget, perhaps now is the right time to touch on a related topic, which is the obesity epidemic in Western countries. Obesity is so common today that there is now a movement to kindly "respect" overweight people. It is "politically incorrect" to call them what they usually are, namely fat, lazy and gluttonous! In extreme cases this leads to them carrying their big bellies proudly in front of them as if it were the most normal thing in the world.

Yes, once a man weighing almost four hundred pounds was mad at me because the seat next to him in the plane wasn't empty but had me in it!

Apart from the damage to their own health, and the damage to the general public due to health care costs – there's another aspect you won't read about anywhere, which I have successfully hidden: **No one who has eaten his way to excess weight can have genuine, sustained self-esteem deep down in his soul.** Deep inside, he is aware of his lack of self-love and self-discipline, and that lack controls his thinking and acting like a slow poison. Outwardly, this inner truth usually hides behind a thick veil of lust for power, self-loathing, sluggish lethargy, as artificial permanent friendliness, self-pity, constant irritability, unpredictability – and all that in any combination and form. Are fat people proud of their big bellies and do they consider them part of their "identity"? No - that is never the case deep down. Anyway, enough of that.

I'm going to take twice as many tennis lessons from now on … Speaking of health: you didn't have anything to do with the Covid-19 epidemic, did you? I'm guessing not, because some church representative or other tried to convince us the pandemic was

"God's punishment". One politician even wanted to use it to further his right-wing extremist agenda, saying it was God's punishment for same-sex marriages and the legalization of abortion.

I have already said everything about it. No, you have yourselves to blame for this epidemic. Question: why did eighty per cent of the Native Americans die when the first white settlers arrived in North America?

Because they weren't vaccinated?

Do you think joking about this is appropriate?

Oops, sorry, no. I guess they weren't immune to the little creatures the settlers brought with them: viruses, bacteria …

Right. Just like few people were immune to Covid-19, which spread through animals without harming them. Viruses mutate all the time, and if you're foolish enough to consider their host animals a delicacy, then they can spread like wildfire. You have been playing with fire for a long time. You can read about the consequences in history books and in cemeteries. I did not have to help there.

So the virus didn't escape from a laboratory somewhere?

No comment. I'll just say this much: it will take decades before you dare to look behind the scenes of this event. And you won't like what you see.

Hmmm, many have experienced this time as an ultimately positive learning experience and have rearranged their everyday life since then. I'm fascinated by how quickly nature has recovered from the overexploitation caused by our permanent consumer frenzy. When dolphins are frolicking again in front of St. Mark's Square in Venice, there is hardly a clearer sign, is there? Or that mountain lakes are filling up again because they no longer have to serve as snow cannon fodder. These are only symptoms, but their meaning is obvious.

The word "crisis" comes from the ancient Greek and means "decision, chance".

During the strict lockdowns I often told a little story as a consolation, which I'm sure you already know:

> *Once upon a time, there was a woman walking in the forest when a small forest spirit met her. "Hey," the forest spirit called out, "I notice that you can see me. For this I grant you a wish." "Hmm," said the woman, "well, the only thing I can think of at this moment is that I always wanted to know the difference between heaven and hell."*

There was a "poof!", and the little forest spirit took the woman by the hand and led her to a wood cabin that appeared before them out of nowhere. They entered it and went through the first door on the left.

A strange scene unfolded in front of them: around a huge round table, many people were sitting trying to eat from delicious food that was piled up in the middle of the table. Their efforts were in vain, because the long cutlery with which they were trying to reach the distant bowls was firmly attached to their hands. They were not able to bring the food to their mouths and seemed completely desperate, as if they were on the verge of starvation.

"This is hell," the forest spirit said. He took the woman by the hand and led her into the room next door.

And behold, an identical scene opened up in front of the eyes of the woman: a huge, round table, people trying to eat under the same conditions from bowls full of delicacies in the middle of the table, several feet away. Only the general atmosphere was completely different: the people were happy, laughing and telling each other stories – and feeding each other effortlessly.

"This is heaven," the forest spirit said.

Yes, that's a useful description of "hell". This crisis, just like any other, was also a subtle nudge to do things differently in all areas in the future. Above all, you should consider ending your meat eating habit once and for all. This was the origin of almost all pandemics in the course of history. However, if you're not careful, the sorcerer´s apprentices in the genetic engineering labs will soon overtake the natural origins of mutated and dangerous viruses.

That's what I´ve always suspected - poisoners, the lot of them! But something that occurred to me in connection with the Covid-19 pandemic was that an idea whose time has come may at first glance seem very small and insignificant – like, for example, Greta Thunberg, a schoolgirl who sat in front of the Swedish parliament with a sign instead of attending classes. What did it say? "School strike for the climate"?

Right. Yes, a virus is very tiny but very powerful. A thought is even smaller, but even more powerful. That is just another truth from which I have successfully "protected" you. Pardon the irony.

In this context, the subject of vaccination comes to my mind immediately. I have always suspected that vaccinations, and even more so compulsory vaccinations, are symptoms of an attitude, a philosophy directed against nature. A philosophy that sees nature as an enemy that must be controlled and dominated.

I've actually already said everything about this. You can establish your own opinion and find the right path. Most importantly you assume responsibility for the path, whichever you might choose.

Maybe this much can be said just so you remember: vaccination means giving the immune system *no* chance to develop and boost itself by its own efforts. You all know that childhood diseases that have been delayed into adulthood create a much greater stress on the body. Childhood diseases are very important for your development, not in themselves but in how you deal with them. You used to know this, and children were sent to school or outside not earlier than three full days after their last fever-free day. Today, you have antibiotics for humans and animals, so you no longer give your faithful vehicle, your body, a chance to defend itself on its own. Very stressful for your bodies, very profitable for the manufacturers. It'll take many decades until independent scientists are able to prove that many diseases of civilization have their origin in the long-term effects of certain vaccines.
And have you already considered why vaccination advocates and supporters are reacting so hysterically to vaccination opponents? After all, they and their children are vaccinated, meaning protected. So what do they have to be afraid of? Why the panic?

I´ve asked myself that too. But I suspect that vaccines are simply a gigantic business for the pharmaceutical industry. They thrive on fear.

Just take a look at who in your country has the right to draw up vaccination plans and present them to politicians for signing. All over the world, the same "experts" sit on the boards of Monsanto, Bayer, Pfizer, Novartis, etc., and everywhere they are playing with the fears and concerns of the parents of small children, to train and drill them to consider vaccination as the duty of every good mother.

You have to realize, as soon as possible, that there is no disease, no pandemic, no plague of pests and weeds, no climate change, no natural disaster that does not have a logical, tangible meaning. All these obstacles invite you to understand them, to understand their *language*. Only then can you create conditions and circumstances that keep such events within limits, or even render them superfluous. Satisfied with this explanation?

Another one of your inducements to stop burying my head in the sand.

You said it! But I see you´ve taken some more notes?

Yes, something a bit crazy and off-field … I've always had the feeling that stand-up comedians have a positive, inspiring influence on the audience. Not for nothing are they feared by politicians. Lenny Bruce comes to mind … How do you go about messing up their work?

Feared by authorities? Hardly at all these days! stand-up comedians rarely have a deep-reaching moral compass and mock many a valuable truth.
I didn't hinder them, I encouraged and promoted them wherever I could, because indirectly they work in accordance with my plans. Open your eyes - usually the people targeted by these comedians sit in the front row shrieking with laughter! Unless they are really dumb and don't get the dynamics because of their ego and false pride. But the butts of the jokes are well aware that wit, cynicism, irony and sarcasm can't hurt them. On the contrary: stand-up comedy was one of my most ingenious inventions!

You created it? How can this be an obstacle on our way? What harm do they do, after all?

That's a question of psychomechanics. Briefly, the same energy that makes the audience laugh, and which seems to have a liberating effect, simultaneously creates the illusion that something has been done to change the lampooned conditions. But that is just a delusion, because nothing has really happened. The trick for me: this illusion reduces the probability of anything being set in liberating motion. You pat each other on the shoulder, wink at one another and say: "Pretty daring, wasn't he?" And that's that.

One of my specialties was to make people laugh in situations where cooperation, mutual help, listening – and helping hands – would have been more appropriate. All too often, laughter is a clear sign of insensitivity. What's so funny about a trampoline jumper bouncing over a hedge and breaking a leg? I was a pro at hiding insensitivity behind a cheerful façade. But "laughing at" and "laughing about" are worlds apart. Want a devil hack here?

A man is being chased by a wild tiger. When the tiger has almost caught up with him and wants to tear him apart, the man jumps into a chasm. At the last moment, he can grab hold of a root five to six feet below the edge which slowly begins to break off. Above him, the wild tiger and the breaking root. Below him, the yawning abyss and certain death. Right next to him, on a tiny rock ledge, a flower. The man reaches out for it, smells it and says: "What beautiful fragrance!"

Oh, please! You've thoroughly spoiled the fun of stand-up comedy and "funny" video shows for many readers now!

My goodness, it's so simple, after all: **just put yourself in the shoes of the person you're laughing at!**

Empathy, my friend, that's it! A long-term solution to the widespread lack of empathy would be to put your kids on bicycles after graduation and pack them off on a trip around the world for a whole year. Mandatory! Then I wouldn't need to have any more conversations like this one. My opportunities to obstruct humanity would diminish to such an extent that I wouldn't have to worry about my job security today.

You're right. I've always thought that happy, liberating laughter and morbid gloating and schadenfreude were as far apart as day and night.

Correct; I always used to take care that the difference remained hidden. Any more questions?

Just an observation: yes, it's true that, in our country, the target audience of cabaret artists often sit in the front row and laugh at the ridiculing of their own inadequacies. But in many countries there are plenty of humorless people at the helm. Just one joke out of place, and you risk being beheaded.

The equation is: the more arrogant, the more humorless. But we don't need to go into that now, the connections are obvious. So: any more questions?

Yes, for sure. Let's look at my notes. Wait … I almost overlooked it, but it is so important – the school system all over the world! As a victim of the system in my youth, I often had the feeling that the devil himself must have come up with the grading system used in school.

You're right. With my help, schools have been turned into an instrument to create as many spiritual prisons as possible; very praiseworthy, your insight. Do you know the movies "The Dead Poets Society", or "Stand and Deliver"? You no idea of the amount of effort and sweat it took to neutralize the positive effects of these movies!
Well, I'll tell you how we went about it: almost all over the world, special interest groups decide on the content of textbooks in schools, and on how teachers are trained, what they have to teach, and in what way. And what are these interests?

Well, their own.

Exactly. So history is falsified, real science is ignored, and instead, political and fanatical religious ideas are promulgated. Unbiased curiosity is killed off or directed into channels that preserve the system. Over fifty per cent of all US-American students haven't even heard of Hitler by the time they leave school.

I'm aware of that.

Do you also understand the grave consequences? The seduction methods of the thimble gang always follow exactly the same procedures – a timeless and easily learnt system that all demagogues know and use. I taught it to them, that was one of my tasks. It is not difficult to see through and describe the system, many of your psychologists and philosophers have already done so. Arno Gruen, for example, was a master at revealing its intricacies. But often there is a strong interest on the part of authority figures to keep the methods of brainwashing secret. Why not, after all? If the future slaves were taught about it in elementary school, they'd be given the key to freedom. Hey, and many teachers would look in the mirror and realize that they were not above using these methods. So they cannot become common knowledge. That's why you can't hold out against them. You will remain victims of the Pied Piper. That was very effective for me – but at the same time, of course, it's one of the reasons why I am talking to you today.

Hmmm, I think I know these methods because I, too, was susceptible to them at certain times of my life. Not a glorious chapter in my career, because today I know how these guys work. At the same time, of course, I've experienced how hard it is to see through their methods.

Don't be too hard on yourself, because back then you were eager for the merchandise in the little shops of horrors of the seducers. Your belated insight that you were just wasting your time is an achievement worthy of respect. Some people babble on about a "necessary step in their development" when they keep running into the same dead ends. Hidden pride and vanity prevent them from changing direction completely .

Thanks for the praise, but I'm still not particularly proud of it. After all, it was a long stretch of delusion.

Enough self-criticism, better late than never. In summary: not exposing the methods of the thimble gang and their followers and making them common knowledge leads to exactly the catastrophe I'm trying to prevent today with your help. You'll have to catch up a lot and quickly to subdue the spirits I have summoned. You also have to realize that the saying "The wiser man retreats" won't help you in the present situation. There could hardly be a more welcoming invitation to the tyrants of the world. If you always lived according to this maxim, soon only complete idiots would be in power.

"The wiser man retreats"! My son first made me aware of the destructive power of this saying. We think far too little about the meaning and value of proverbs!

I've always thought that the best way of dealing with physical and mental violence was one of the biggest problems for all good-natured and good-willed people. You don't want to lower yourself to the same moral level as the aggressors in defending yourself, but you have to find a lasting way to incapacitate them. I'm convinced that anyone who perceives or is exposed to violence and does nothing to stop it, is partly to blame for what later results from the violence.

A wanderer asked the shepherd: "Well, what will the weather be like today?"
The shepherd said: "Just the way I like it." – "How can you tell? By the shape of the clouds?"
"It's been my experience, my friend, that I can't always get what I want. So I have learned to always like what I get. That's why I'm sure: the weather today will be just the way I like it."

This dilemma is one of the greatest challenges you will encounter in this world. There are no blanket solutions. The extremes of correct behavior oscillate between "turning the other cheek" and "an eye for an eye and a tooth for a tooth", with many other options in between.

I remember a friend avoiding a fight with an aggressive bar bully by faking a heart attack.

That is an ingenious maneuver! But! Only if it *actually* turns out to be successful in any given situation. This behavior is inappropriate as general advice - on another day, the thug might have kicked your friend lying on the ground and smashed his skull in. There is no panacea!

Oops, I hadn't even thought of that possibility ... Speaking of dealing with violence: I remember the example of a girlfriend. A contact agreement after her divorce forced her to hand over her four-year-old son to her ex-husband every other weekend – he being a very unpleasant person, to put it mildly. Her son was always irritated and disturbed after these weekends and needed days to recover. Finally my girlfriend simply stopped the visits, also because her son didn't want to see his father anymore either. A family judge ordered her to do everything she could to coerce her son to see his father "voluntarily". My girlfriend then asked him straight to his face: "So you want to force me to lie through my teeth to my son and dismiss his traumatic experiences with my ex-husband as imagination or delusion?" The judge was actually stunned.

I remember. Your girlfriend can consider herself lucky, because most judges are men who have no understanding for so much insight and personal responsibility on the part of a woman. Certainly they do not respect the child's perception.

I've experienced that, too. I accompanied my girlfriend through all the legalities of right of access and contact. There were even several court-appointed psychologists and consultants who wanted to force her to leave her child with its father. And there was another, completely twisted family judge who tried to convince her that it was good for the child's welfare to visit the alcoholic father regularly because "then he can experience right away what real life is like". Later it turned out that the judge himself was an alcoholic.

Well what a surprise ... As I said, you don't learn anything about connections like these in schools, and certainly not what a correct and humane approach to negativity might look like. You don't learn anything about the unfolding of free will and a genuine desire to explore. You learn nothing about sex (except its mechanics) and nothing about the healthy handling of money as a form of energy, which is so important! You cannot release your natural urge to move, even at the very time when it is most necessary, and when you feel that urge most strongly.
You learn nothing about the harmony at the core of all religions, which would render all external differences meaningless. You learn nothing about physical, mental and spiritual independence. You learn nothing about true joy of life and its true sources. And you learn nothing about choosing a profession wisely to follow your calling – something that schools should provide at least.

Right, that was exactly my own experience. Because my family moved house several times, I had about fifty teachers, professors, etc. in my life. I remember exactly four of them with real delight, they really left their mark. Strangely enough, years ago I visited one of them, my old gym teacher, for the first time since my school days, almost forty years later. Imagine, he told me that I was the first student from back then to pay him a visit. I was stunned and close to tears, because at that moment I felt ashamed for all mankind.

Today the situation seems to be much better, from what I hear when I listen to my children and their experiences. But many teachers today have the problem of not being sufficiently prepared to deal with large numbers of disturbed, violent children.

So I think you're right: the poor state of our school system is primarily a matter of training. Teachers, however well-intentioned, are not thoroughly prepared for the realities in class. Good intentions don't amount to anything without the necessary tools to make them work.

From talking to you so far, I also realize why good teachers never had a chance in the past to climb up the career ladder in the school system. Those higher-up would have to open the doors to someone lower-down, and this would increase the perceived danger that a competent newcomer would discover what they were made of and what their intentions really were – namely, to make us all "normal". After all, it's just the same in politics and often also in the economy.

Well diagnosed. Of course, young trainee teachers have no idea of the extent to which they'll be hemmed in by rigid pedagogical methods. They discover only gradually, when they are open to it, that school is a great distraction that focuses on anything but the essentials in life.

Everyday life in the teaching profession is tough. It's anything but the walk in the park with lots of vacations that outsiders suspect. Teachers at all-day schools, for example, both the good and the "normal" ones, are almost scared of the hours after lunch. School lunches make kids irritable and tired, they stuff them with empty calories. Which brings me back to the subject of normal nutrition.

I intimated that meat, dairy and sugar are necessary basic foods, and had a good laugh when you became tired, irritable and obnoxious after "enjoying" these things – yet you still fall for the advertising slogans of the manufacturers of "Stuff-bloat-fillers" to this day.

I've only recently realized that sugar is not a basic food.

A question for you: what is the difference between a poison that kills you after a few minutes, and a poison that slowly weakens you more and more and makes you sick until it kills you after twenty years?

I'd have to think about it … One difference would certainly be whether you ingested the poison unintentionally, for example as an Amazon explorer who caught the poison of a poison dart frog, or whether someone had administered it intending to kill.

Okay, and what about the difference between immediate death or only after twenty years?

I'm certain that if I could convince a judge that the poison which would kill me after twenty years was intentionally mixed into my food, the killer would serve a life sentence … I think.

Okay, and now remember how many billions of dollars the tobacco industry had to pay in compensation when it was proved that it deliberately made smokers sick.

Right, that finally almost succeeded in putting a stop to the killers.

And now take a look at the food industry and the sugar industry in particular. They poison you on purpose, don't they? They all know what sugar does to the body; they all know what meat and dairy do to the body, not to mention the environmental damage in the course of production. The tobacco and food industries are drug dealers. The goal is to get you addicted to their products, not to "feed the world's population". Example? What proportion of the world's total grain production is fed to livestock in factory farming? What do you think?

Twenty per cent?

Two thirds. By how much would your meat consumption have to decrease in order to eliminate all hunger in the world with the farmland gained?

By half?

By ten per cent. How many people can be fed with planting grain on a quarter of an acre farmland? Ten. How many people can be fed by a quarter of an acre livestock pasture?

Well, if you ask like that, certainly a few less.

Just one. How long can you take a shower with the drinking water needed to produce two pounds of beef?

Ten days?

A whole year. I know these interrelationships very well, and that's why I exported milk powder and wheat to suffering populations in the Third World, to disaster areas, etc. Both foods are empty and make you sick and dependent. That was very important to me because often the people in these countries used to live on a very healthy diet without animal protein. Take Mexico for example: until twenty years ago, everyone there lived primarily on beans and corn tortillas, but today Mexico has the highest consumption of sugared soda pops. And packaged wheat toast bread without any nutritional value has replaced the corn tortillas. Today, Mexico is the country with the highest increase in obesity and diabetes.

This was even reported by the mainstream media …

You know now: nothing played more into my hands than dependence and exhaustion, mental and physical. That was my goal! But only up to exhaustion, not to

self-destruction! That´s why we are talking to each other today.
"The meat industry is responsible for more deaths than all wars of the last century, all natural disasters and all car accidents together. If, in your mind, meat means "real food for real men", then you should take care to live really close

One day, a master asked his students how they can distinguish the end of the night from the beginning of the day.
One student said: "If you see an animal in the distance and can distinguish whether it is a cow or a horse."
"No," said the master.
"If you can see from a distance and recognize whether the tree is a cherry or a peach tree."
"Wrong again," said the master.
"If you can see from a distance whether it's a bird or a bat that flies."
"No, not either," said the teacher.
"Well, how then?" asked the students.
"If one looks into the face of a man and recognizes in it the brother; if one looks into the face of a woman and recognizes in her the sister. Whoever is not able to do so, for him there is night – wherever the sun may stand."

to a really good hospital." That is what one of your leading doctors recently said …

Speaking of "real men eat real meat": a scientific study found that in men who live on a plant-based diet, spontaneous night erections were four times longer and much more "stable" than in men with a normal diet. I recommend the documentary "The Game Changers". Available on Netflix.

I know the study and the film, and in my current situation I can only recommend them as well! Any other questions?

Let me take a quick look at my notes … What other tricks do you have up your sleeve?

How about this one? At all times, one of my strongest weapons has been to subject people to a form of brainwashing that resulted in them seeing progress in painting the bars of their prison. You know the most popular saying of this slave mentality: "We have always done it this way." Second most popular: "Why? I'm free to do as I please!"

Hm, perhaps the readers should google the term "Stockholm Syndrome".

Good suggestion. By the way, chronic fatigue is an important way of making sure that no one wakes up to the reality of their own situation. Competitive thinking is also an important factor; I encouraged it wherever I could, even in schools. Nowadays it is almost impossible to find students who are willing to let their fellow students take a peek at their own tests and notes.

Tell me about it! I was lucky, and my best friend, who was talented in mathematics and Latin, always let me have a look. The Native Americans grew up differently, by the way. New students in the reservation often turned in blank papers for written exams, even though they were well prepared. They didn't want to out-perform those classmates who couldn't solve the tasks they were given. Just a thought … Competitive thinking then merges seamlessly into business life, into professional everyday life.

Right. Although "team spirit" is emphasized so markedly almost everywhere, it is hardly practiced at all. More or less hidden hierarchies are almost always at work, and companies often function like small kingdoms. They no longer see success in cultivating guest and customer care and a high-quality product, but in "more, more, more". Everywhere "growth at any cost" is the order of the day, whereas friendly concern for guests, customers and products is a "necessary evil" and an annoying "cost factor". This attitude is so ingrained that genuine cooperation and unconditional giving are almost automatically met with distrust – or at least with the feeling: "what return favor is now expected, to what extent and when?"

Oh, now that you mention it: in my travels in the West, I have noticed more and more often that a small present is perceived almost as subtle blackmail, because my host asks himself: "What does he want from me? What favor is expected from me in return?"

Yes, giving is sometimes easier than taking. In the business world, you'll notice that it's a law of nature: everything that aspires to grow big or has grown big – companies, corporations, hotel chains etc. – has only become so for one reason: greed. Never to provide a service for the customers. Their number one concern is to make customers dependent on their own products, only by legal means, of course: addictive ingredients loyalty points, company credit cards, advertising slogans and much more. Essentially, these companies are small cogs in a drug industry machine. That is why the employees of such ever-expanding hot air balloons are not employees, colleagues, associates, but slaves who must be exploited in a more or less shameless way to keep prices down.

Almost every company above a certain size is now a mini-tyranny with a tight hierarchy, and almost all of them are among the listed companies. In the USA, seventy-eight per cent of all workers live from monthly salary to monthly salary without being able to save any money.

Clearly visible during the Covid pandemic …

You want a job as a chambermaid at the Hilton? Your manual for correct rules of conduct is two inches thick. Family with two children? You'll need two full-time jobs just to make ends meet, without being able to add to a savings account. Successful devil hack: **only buy real quality, and only from small companies, and ideally only work for them too – the more local, the better.**

Well, I see a contradiction there. If this greedy striving for expansion is, or was, also in your interests, that is, if you at least initially encouraged it until it developed into the cancerous growths we see today, how does that fit in with your intention to encourage laziness and lethargy, as one of your essential tasks?

Deep down in the sea
immeasurable treasures lie hidden.
Security and safeguards
you find on the shore.
(Oriental wisdom)

There's no contradiction, hence these examples, although we've talked about them before. Here, the laziness refers to rigid concepts, such as "the economy needs continuous growth". *A humane and compassionate world economy needs nothing less than this deadly ideology!* Your economy needs thinking and acting in natural cycles, it needs harmony with the real needs of humans, animals and nature. Monsanto, Nestlé, Exponent, Bayer and the many other companies that do not heed this – they have always been on *my* side. Just like the eighty-five per cent of all scientists who are paid by them and cook up what you can rightly call "Fake Science". Would you like an example of one of my most loyal followers?

Gladly. The more eye openers for the readers, the better!

Question: which company was commissioned by the meat industry to produce studies that prove that meat is *not* unhealthy?

Aha, paid science …

It is the same company that proved to you that tobacco does not cause cancer, that asbestos and sugar are harmless, and that glyphosate and all other pesticides pose no health risk. Its name is Exponent Inc., and they specialize in helping big industry every time injured parties fight against companies. Exponent´s main mission is to sow doubt – in personal experience, common sense and independent scientific studies that would be helpful to the plaintiffs.

"In dubio pro reo," right? When in doubt, find for the accused. I've always thought that while this legal principle is a protection for innocent defendants, it's probably just as often a loophole for the bad guys, because sowing doubt is no problem for a good lawyer.

Right, and almost all big companies are among Exponent´s clients – Monsanto, Dow Chemicals, oil companies, the sugar industry, etc. Many people have to get sick and die before the truth prevails. Exponent has overtaken me, they are better than me today.

Never heard of the company, but I'm sure that's no wonder, because today almost all media rely on industry commercials. They'll be wary of permitting any glimpses behind-the-scenes …

All you have to do is read between the lines on Exponent´s website. The devil hack here is that you realize the following: *when you take something from a supermarket shelf, you create a vacuum into which the exact same product is sucked.* If you leave it there, it won't be reordered. Simple, isn't it? You don't practice real democracy at the polling station. You practice it in front of the shelves in the stores. You determine what the shelves are filled with and which companies have a chance. This decision is of greater consequence than any electoral decision in politics.

I haven't bought Nestlé products for a long time. Oh well.

I think I need to make myself clearer. The individual has the power, not the politicians. It's what you buy that changes the world, not your vote in elections. You buy a T-shirt for five dollars? You just have prolonged the suffering of women in Asia´s sweatshops. You buy a bottle of water from Nestlé or any of the other water robbers? You just have helped to exploit the wonderful blessing of water and turn it into stinking ponds and deserts. You get electricity from coal, oil and nuclear power? You bring the earth not just one but several steps closer to the last shrug of her shoulders with which she'll shake you all off and start anew. Whether the earth is the paradise for which it is intended, or whether she'll buck you off like a wild horse does, you have it in your own hands – every single one of you.

Ouch, strong stuff … But even so I have the feeling that you're right.

Your miners, your oil workers, your nuclear engineers – you could easily and in a short time retrain them to become forest workers, forest caretakers and forest engineers, and they would, from then on, have hardly any problems with their lungs and with radiation.

A pipe dream - but what about the countless women workers in Bangladesh, India and elsewhere, if the clothing factories had to close? A common argument against not buying cheap products from such countries is that valuable jobs would be lost there ...

Utter nonsense. That's an argument spread by those who have an interest in maintaining the status quo. The people in such countries have the ability to meet these challenges. You call that "resilience" today. Secondly, it would be no problem to reduce the dependence on exports of these countries by turning their attention to conditions in their own countries. In addition, you could make up a little for what your exploitation has done, with meaningful aid programs for once. Help for self-help is the keyword.
Have you ever asked yourself why many people from Central and South America want to emigrate, although their own countries are true paradises in terms of landscape and nature?

I have. I have a feeling they do it because they've been seduced by television, Western lifestyle and advertising, to believe that the grass is greener on the other side of the fence. They no longer want to be poor peasants but would prefer to get the "comforts of progress". From dish washer to millionaire, or something of that sort. And of course, they are also fleeing the chaos caused by those in power in their own countries.

Correct, and take your time now to ask yourself what it means when someone here complains and whines about the high number of immigrants. And about them taking away your jobs.

I can only laugh at such BS! Wherever people complain about that, hardly any native is willing to do the jobs that are taken on by immigrants. The hatred for immigrants is artificially fueled by populists who don't think from here to the next doorpost and rely on the votes of the uneducated.

Correct. And I'll be even more clear: even though I was the king of slowing things down, of stagnation, of crystallization, you wouldn't necessarily recognize my success by the increasing number of couch potatoes, overweight people and TV dinners sold. Outwardly, a person can be in fast motion and at a hectic pace, he can build companies, win empires, Olympic gold medals, he can even start wars and appear on television three times a day – and still be among my victims. Namely, when the outer restlessness is a symptom of inner rigidity, a rigid set of beliefs, an ideology, a fixed delusion. Fruitful movement and genuine development are often not so easy to identify from the outside. Laziness can hide behind hectic activism. To fight a forest fire, it would suffice to *not* throw away the burning cigarette, instead of waiting for the fifty helicopters and the five hundred firefighters.

Okay, I think I get it now. Moving on, what else is there that you are behind without anyone suspecting it?

The tax deductibility of charitable donations as well as the rebate and discount system in your global economy.

Excuse me? You can't be serious!

What great fortune –
the diversity of people!
Because only then do
four eyes see more than two.
(The Translator)

Believe me, those were clever moves. It is undoubtedly true that giving is more blessed than receiving. A truly generous nature, or a basic attitude of sharing among brothers and sisters in the world, can make a person immune to my influence. But only when the giving is done *anonymously* and without any expectation of a favor in return. The mere gratitude of the recipient, let alone the possibility of reducing one's own tax burden through donations, transforms giving into a trade, into an investment. I give, I get in return: money, flattery, gratitude, the feeling of being "good", etc. Only when you give like a flower that can't help but spread its fragrance, does giving have a very special, uplifting effect. This I had to neutralize.

Another line of thought that I will think about a lot. We once anonymously helped a neighboring family that had lost everything after a fire in their home, because my wife wanted us to. I remember that was a special feeling ... And what's so bad about the rebate and discount system? Well, I can guess, though ...

It's obvious, isn't it? A bank picks a company it wants to grow, and against all common sense and without a credit check, hands out a big loan, mostly because the bankers themselves are profiting under the table. You know, bonuses and awards, and so on ... This loan now enables the company to buy large quantities of a product because of the discount system – the more you buy of a product, the cheaper you'll get it. This allows the shark in the corporate carp tank to wipe out smaller competitors using the apparent "price advantage". The banks get fat, the big companies even fatter, and so do the shareholders without lifting a finger. And all this in the short and long term at the expense of product quality and customer friendliness. The rebate and discount system is the number one quality killer and a destroyer of diversity.

And at the expense of compassion in dealing with big company employees, I might add. I've arrived at precisely the same observations and experiences in dealing with large companies, hotel and restaurant chains, etc. Okay, what other arrows are in your quiver?

A seemingly quite incidental decision that I inspired.

I'm curious already. Let me guess: probably it has to do with cell phones and tablets and PCs, and with the fact that everyone gets hypnotized by flickering screens these days. Or now you're telling me that you invented Wikipedia and its draconian rules about what is supposed to be counted as authentic and correct, and what isn't. Wikipedia even went so far as to not allow a superstar writer to add personal experience to his entry. There would be no "proof" for it, he was told.

You´re close. No, right now I'm talking about the decision to allow *anonymous* posting in the Internet chat rooms of media, newspapers, in comment functions, social media applications, Twitter, etc. Of course, today I view my achievements with mixed feelings, because it has taken you a big step further towards the abyss. In fact, I would've never expected such a huge success.

With some things, I just initiate them, and I don't immediately realize what I've done.

Hmmm, at the moment I don´t see what should have been so super destructive about it.

Open your eyes, for Buddy´s sake! Suppose you have a thousand fans for one of your books and one envious hater among the reviews. Who does the media highlight? Who is the attention focused on? Who is your *personal* attention focused on? Who is gaining "weight"? Observe, make your own judgment! Next, observe the simultaneous dropping of moral taboos, the rising propensity for violence, the increasingly black-and-white thinking, the growing courage to "let it all hang out" verbally. Trump wanted to build walls, but in reality he tore down walls that had kept the flows of hatred at bay so far. The damage done by this person is immeasurable, because he removed moral barriers in every corner of the world. And that was possible precisely because hate was able to spread as a cancer in social media – primarily because of anonymity! Compare media that allow anonymous comments with media where you have to register with a real name beforehand. You can tell them apart by the smell of sulfur.

You've convinced me. When I read the reviews of my books on Amazon, I spend more time with the harsh critics and think about how I can win them over.
OK, can we turn to a marginal topic that I feel very strongly about? I have written a lot on the subject of popular medicine and helping people to help themselves. Herbalism is one of the hobbies in my family, to the point of building herbal stone spirals in our gardens. What I find appalling is the way modern medicine deals with folk medicine. Recently, a scientist claimed that it is not true that there is an herb for every disease, and that we therefore need genetic engineering. He dares to claim this although only ten per cent of all plants in the world have been tested for their healing powers – something this quack knows full well! I think we should not attempt to interfere with Buddy by genetically manipulating plants. Man has not even begun to understand nature, let alone to gratefully accept all its gifts. What should genetic engineering be called then? In my opinion, its proponents and advocates seem to resemble people who fall from the thirtieth floor, and who, on their way down, say: "Everything has gone well so far!" Fortunately, we do not have to be used as guinea pigs. We always have a democratic choice at the grocery store.

Well roared, little lion. Yes, the thing about the "crown of creation" and "dominion over the earth," you have thoroughly misunderstood, with my assistance, of course. Take a look at the USA: the drug industry here – legal as well as illegal – has succeeded in making almost every American addicted to drugs; from aspirin, which doctors recommend to be taken daily, to painkillers which are prescribed for many decades until they tear the liver and kidneys to pieces (and make even more pills necessary). "A healthy person just hasn't been examined closely enough," is what an American general practitioner once said. Over sixty per cent of all Americans take medications on a daily basis. And if a company drug peddler complains about slowing sales of its cholesterol medication, their lobbyist is immediately sent out to inspire the responsible authority to have the threshold value for what is considered "healthy" lowered. And suddenly everyone needs this stuff. Ingenious, isn't it?

Well, I have a different idea of what to call "ingenious"!

All birds, even those of the same species, are not alike,
and it is the same with animals and with human beings.
The reason Buddy does not make two birds, or animals, or human beings exactly alike is because each is placed here by Buddy to be an independent individuality and to rely upon itself. (Teton-Sioux)

May I comfort you with a secret for yourself and your readers? Perhaps you can turn off your inner turmoil with a short meditation before you listen further. Because I'm going to reveal a secret, the implications of which cannot be overstated. A super devil hack that will let you get closer to Buddy automatically. I have worked for many centuries to make this secret disappear from your collective memory. But now it's time for you to reflect on it again.

I'm listening …

Imagine the following scenario in your mind's eye: a family of parents and three kids lives in a single-family house, some way out in the suburbs. They have decided, for whatever reason, to leave a small area of about ten by ten feet in their garden to grow wild. Over time, a small, beautiful wilderness emerges, a micro jungle full of wild flowers, grasses, herbs and weeds …
And now imagine that family moves out, and a new family moves in. The new residents kind of like the idea of the mini jungle and leave it as it is. They only trim it once a year, they don't plant anything, they don't fertilize or care for the plants. Instead of artificial garden "culture" they watch how a mix of small herbs and flowers develops. Exactly as the previous family treated the patch. So what happens now, after the new family moves in? Listen carefully: **the composition of the**

plant family changes all by itself. The herbs that settle in are exactly those that the new family needs to stay and become healthy: dandelion, nettles, celandine, daisies, etc. Sometimes also yellow dead-nettle, small-flowered willow herb and other rather rare herbs which are often also considered weeds. A mix of plants, as specific to the new family as the previous combination of plants was to the previous owners.

Is this actually the case?

Yes, nature has responded to the family – Buddy has responded to that family. She sends precisely those plants that are meant for this family, and thus often reveals previously undetected diseases or weaknesses.
Think about this fact for a moment. What has happened here? What language does nature speak? And why don't you learn about it in schools, from the media, from science? What intention does this silence stand for, why ignore it? The question about the meaning of life knows several valid and true answers. One of them can be felt acutely if you reflect and meditate on facts like these. Just ask yourself what this information actually means for the world. What does it mean when you still mistranslate the Bible and misunderstand Genesis 1/16 "dominion over the earth"?

I just think that we are meant to work in harmony with nature, not to exploit it.

Right. Any kind and loyal servant turns into a cold-blooded rebel when he is degraded into a slave, as is the case with your genetic engineers.

What exactly is wrong with genetic engineering? I feel it is an aberration of science, and I think it turns all of us into guinea pigs because there is not a single long-term study of the consequences. But I have a hard time arguing when I'm dealing with a supporter.

Why argue? Your counterpart is invariably mimicking beliefs, not knowledge. So what exactly would be your intention in the conversation? A compromise in the exchange of beliefs? Genetic engineering exists only because most scientists have completely lost touch with nature and trust in it, or never had it. On top of that, there is a secure, high-paying job and the prospect of medals and decorations, a lot of prestige. The truth is, genetic engineering … Well, I have an analogy for that. Interested?

I can´t wait, tell me!

Imagine a very wonderful pocket watch, made by the best watchmaker of his time. It is a marvel of craftsmanship, a gift for the king. It even shows the position of the moon in the zodiac, it has been running for a hundred years and hardly needs any care and maintenance. Now imagine that the knowledge of how to maintain this clock has been lost, as the last watchmaker died without passing on his skills. The clock has therefore stopped one day. The servants of the current king see no other solution than to command the best artisan blacksmith of the country to repair the clock. Loaded with his forging tools, he visits the king's court and sets to work with the best of intentions, primarily using large hammers of different sizes. Do you think he will make the clock work? Will he improve it?

That's exactly my feeling. Sorcerer's apprentices, putting our future at risk.

To think for oneself is not selfish. A man who does not think for himself does not think at all.
(Oscar Wilde)

Your misfortune is that some short-term accidental success is achieved in the genetic engineering laboratories, for example in problems with plant pests. That makes for effective advertising. However, in the best symptom-fighting manner, the mass occurrence of pests is viewed in completely the wrong way. Remember the example from earlier when the herbs growing in the garden changed with the new family moving in. So what is Mother Nature trying to tell you when she sends pests en masse?

Looking at it this way, I guess she's telling us, "Get rid of the stuff!"

The fact is, a greenhouse tomato, sprayed with pesticides and artificially fed, is a *sick creature* in the eyes of nature, your guardian! She recognizes the long-term damage you would be doing to yourselves with those red water balls. In her wisdom and generosity, and in the attempt to maintain balance everywhere, the sophisticated immune system of nature sends defensive substances against the disease called "cultivated tomato". Misjudging the context, you call these valuable protective and defensive substances "pests", "weeds" and "plant diseases".
As I said, concerning your way of practicing science, I suggested to your scientists that it is always better to fight problems instead of understanding them. In doing so, I used a trick. Do you have any idea which one?

In an exam I would get an "F" because I don't have the faintest idea.

Some hundred years ago, according to your current calendar, I convinced you that *feelings* have no place in science, and that scientific findings and results are valid only if they can be repeated. My ploy was a runaway success - I could never have guessed how enthusiastically the concept would be received by you people. I was literally driven to tears when I saw how easily many of your scientists stifled their feelings and conscience before they went on to build war machines, invent dynamite, atomic bombs, mass surveillance, pesticides, hybrid seeds and many more such blessings. And with what shocking arrogance they denigrated millennia-old knowledge as "superstition", from the precious knowledge of healing herbs to knowledge about the influence of nature and moon rhythms on all life.

Tell me about it. I remember the scientists on talk shows where I appeared. When they were asked if they'd tried anything we were writing about, the answer was invariably "no".

Yes, these guys are like babies demanding proof that breast milk is good for them before they deign to suckle. And you people, you trust science today more than whatever gifts Buddy has in store for you at any given moment. You are like prisoners hoping to be liberated by their guards. How can you expect liberation from a science that declares the living fundamental force of the human being, namely love, to be something "unscientific", at best controlled by some hormones and chemical processes in the body? Do you know what the crazy thing about this is?

That we're digging our own graves?

No, thank Buddy, we haven't come that far yet. What's crazy is that all scientists without exception embark on their professional life based on completely unscientific *emotions.* How did they decide to take up their profession? How do they decide on certain paths, methods, projects, collaborators, vacation spots, wives, husbands, the names of their children, the color of the curtains, etc.? They may tell themselves as much as they like that "rational considerations" played a part in each case, but it was always emotions that dictated their most important decisions. And perhaps you should ponder the fact that measuring instruments, even today, are called "feelers". All science, without exception, is sensing and feeling! But nevertheless, you decided to discount whole worlds of feeling and emotion and reduce them to a small, cold world without heart.
Want an example? In many regions of the world, companies are out tracking down water wells with the latest sonar technology. They have a success rate of about thirty per cent. There are people who have eighty

per cent success, traveling all alone, using only a dowsing rod as an aid.

I've already seen for myself that pendulums and dowsing rods work. But it's not easy to exclude self-interest if you want to get useful results from them.

No pain, no gain. On the subject of science, two anecdotes that might be useful to your readers: shortly after World War I, a young doctor was working in one of Europe's many overcrowded orphanages. One day he noticed that the infants in a particular ward seemed more cheerful and lively, looked better fed, were less likely to get sick and, in general, were in much better health than all the other children in the same age group. At first, his medical training led the doctor to believe that someone was feeding the children from private stocks in addition to the meager daily rations in the orphanage. After some time, however, he realized that this was not the reason for the children's better condition. Their diet was exactly the same as that of the other children of the same age. The doctor found that there was actually only one difference: unlike the rest of the staff, the caregiver in charge of the hopelessly understaffed orphanage made an "extra effort" to lift each child out of bed before feeding, cradling it in his arms, caressing and stroking it before giving him the bottle and putting it back. Via the skin to the heart – without detours.

I know about this study, but I can't remember where I read it. Perhaps in the book "Job's Body" by Deane Juhan, which I recently had a look at. A wonderful book, by the way! Thanks for the reminder, that's a great example.

The second anecdote: during a study in the 1970s, scientists stuffed rabbits with special concentrated feed to study the development of heart diseases. There were consistent results – with one exception: a certain group of rabbits showed sixty per cent fewer symptoms of the disease! It was only by chance that it was finally discovered that the biology student responsible for feeding this group liked to take "his" rabbits in his arms for a few minutes and caress them lovingly.
Now what consequences has conventional medicine drawn from these lessons? What deduction can you draw from these two examples?

If I were a scientist, I would do absolutely everything to make sure that these observations get the attention they deserve! You've already mentioned the consequences of lack of touch for babies and children. It's absolute madness, the way we're eliminating the heart and common sense from our modern science.

Anyone who retains the ability to see beauty never grows old.

(Franz Kafka)

My friend, the earth wants to be your friend, and you allow it to degenerate into a slave. The earth will not put up with that in the long run. Wonderful nature, in its actual essence, is completely unknown to the vast majority of people. It is experienced as hostile – the mosquito flying in through the window could transmit a disease, the bee or wasp could sting. Whole areas of land and urban regions are routinely sprayed with pesticides from the air. "The strongest survives" – you have wrongly attributed this false observation to your Mr. Charles Darwin. This is contrary to all experience and contrary to all reality in nature. If it were correct, after the many millions of years of evolution, there would be only one species of animals and one species of plants, namely the ones that won the race. Your restaurant menu cards would be very boring to read.

Hey, looking at it that way … But there are many well-intentioned people working as scientists to bring about progress.

Progress? Correct, that's what you have achieved. Instead of using lances and bows and arrows, you can now transport yourselves back to Buddy´s home more quickly and efficiently. Progress does actually exist, but I have convinced you that progress in the quality of your tools is *all the progress you need*! You consider as progress the advancement of your tools and have forgotten that the hand using the tool is much more important when it comes to the question of the real development of humankind. For you, even leaf blowers, lawn mowing robots and microwave ovens mean "progress" – all of them such incredibly foolish and destructive inventions that we always celebrated when your engineers fell for suggestions like these.

And you also consider "increasing speed" as a value in itself. "He may have crashed into the wall, but at least he was going faster than one hundred miles per hour." To have a train going from X to Y arrive five minutes earlier, you spend as much money as would prevent fifteen thousand children a year starving to death, whilst also exterminating many animal and plant species.

You overlook day after day that the heart and hand which *use* the tools must develop and mature! You are like a bunch of children playing in a sandbox who are happy to get real hand grenades to play with instead of water pistols. Applause!

But calm down, I wouldn't be here if there wasn't hope. You have it in your own hands, as in all earlier times …

I see my time here gradually coming to an end; I'd like to give you the opportunity to ask me one or two more questions that are really pressing to you personally.

I've already thought about it, and made a few quick notes. What's really on my mind, of course, because it concerns my children: what's your involvement in social media, Facebook and the like? We've already touched on it, and I think it's apparent to almost everyone that there are forces at work that don't bode well for the world. Real communication, being able to listen, being able to make yourself understood – all of that is suffering, I think. A US American president as a Twitter hate preacher? Where is all this going? Is there something I can do to help, maybe with my writing?

Sure. Just always make sure your work is available on those very social media platforms, as an e-book, online, etc. And always connect with the people where they are: build bridges. Connecting with them was also necessary for me, by the way. I always asked myself, what makes it easier to seduce someone and stop him in his tracks? That's how *I* connected with him.

The advertising industry was actually one of your most successful projects, wasn't it? Man, what a job, I wouldn't want to trade places with you. But I have a couple more questions. On the topic of cell phones, social media, video games and so on, it occurred to me that there is intense discussion today about whether increasing violence is triggered by these media, by video games, etc. I only have to compare my own or my parents' upbringing with the influences my children are exposed to every day. There must be negative effects, even if the media deny it, and even if they cite science as proof.

These effects do exist. By the time children reach the age of eighteen, they've seen an average of one hundred thousand murders on television and in the movies, but no more than ten acts of love as an expression of genuine, tender love. Not counting porn; that's almost always competitive sport, violence and callousness. Almost all your successful online computer games, almost all media, almost all politicians are living examples of what it's like to be under the influence of drugs. Their guiding principles are "solving problems with violence is okay" or "violence brings more clicks and readers than cooperation, conversation and solution" or "willingness to compromise is weakness" or "revenge is a duty of honor". Many of your politicians and media are perfect arsonists in this sense. Scientists, sociologists, etc. were submissive tools who calmed down parents and other people and made them believe that all this violence in the media does not lead to more violence in society. That is as crazy as the belief that rampages and killing sprees in schools can be prevented by arming all students and teachers. Do you remember that hippie motto from the 1960s?

Well, there were many good ones …

I mean this one: "Fighting for peace is like fucking for virginity."

A very convincing adage, and surely an inspiration for many conscientious objectors …

Yes, that was a good one, and therefore not mine. The statistics your scholars fabricate on the subject of "media promotion of violence" should remind you of the saying: "I only believe statistics I've forged myself." Yes, you've been my pliable students, but – for Buddy´s sake and yours – this can't be allowed to continue. Books and films like "The Hut" or people like Dag Hammarskjöld, Yogananda, Arno Gruen, Michael Newton, etc. provide you with living proof that things can be done differently.

May I ask a question that's bothering me personally at the moment?

Go ahead.

I'd be interested to know where you've already met me in the past and led me astray. Honestly, you look familiar to me.

My goodness, I look familiar to *everyone*! But you have been a challenge, indeed. Getting you to waste time in this round wasn't easy because you're a writer who wants to feel he is inspiring his readers. It's hard to lead people like you astray, but I ended up having at least a little success the usual way.

There is a "usual" way with writers?

Sure there is. Just take a look or two at the millions of "how-to" guide books. Almost all of them contain a bibliography in the appendix. That's the list of all the books the author has *copied from*. And right there I have the author, who essentially has only a few sentences of original, new material to offer. But because that's not enough for a whole book, at most for a blog post or maybe just a tweet, he has to collect material, a lot of hot air, and inflate his sentences into a book. Eighty per cent of all nonfiction books are written this way.

Oh dear, I have to confess that´s also true for my first two books …

Exactly, but to keep such scribes in line, I had to work hard, stroke egos, contrive to get them onto a bestseller list, and so on. Otherwise you and many others would have come to the realization much sooner that writing from your own experience gives much more real satisfaction. Only such words have real energy! So why have I distracted you for a long time? Because a writer who writes about something without personal, direct experience of it has no real impact on his readers. In the same way that I steer him in the wrong direction, so he seduces his readers. You can buy hundreds of cookbooks without the author having cooked a single one of his recipes himself. You can feel it, you can taste it! And then you whine about your stomach ache afterwards!

Yes, right, especially the recipes starting with "Preheat the oven…" and **then** *you have to start to prepare the veggies, spices etc. for an hour..*
Okay, I'll calm my nerves now. I've often thought about this. I imagine what would've happened if I'd been very successful with such second-hand work. It would be very embarrassing, having to present your work in interviews or in public, as if everything was your own intellectual authorship. There's nothing worse than being successful with something contrived and unloved, right?

A sparkling gem in my bag of tricks.

What else? How else did you take special care of me?

Something that wasn't difficult, but with serious consequences. It was easy with almost everyone in your situation. It's the matter of your interest in spirituality, in what you call the "new age", in the true meaning of life, in enlightenment, self-realization. Those are interests which are absolutely opposed to my interests, because there is the real danger that you will escape from my influence not only temporarily but *permanently* and *effectively*. So, to ensure that you didn't succeed, I used a tried and tested method which works quickly and permanently with almost all spiritually inclined people.

Well, now I'm all ears.

I ensured that you confused the deep, intense feelings that esoteric exercises and self-awareness methods often trigger, with true insight and spiritual progress.

I had led the vast majority of leaders and followers of such groups, sects, gurus, therapists, etc. to believe that intense emotions, orgiastic climaxes, catharsis, crying fits and moments of intense delight are in themselves signs of "progress". One is convinced then that one has chosen the right path if only one stays long enough with this guru or that method. And the more time and money spent, the deeper the conviction. **Confusing emotion with insight and knowledge, that's the trick.**

Pseudo-Evangelists and most gurus work with this method. I always had a good laugh when I was successful here, because people have overlooked the simplest thing.

And what would be the simplest thing? Just keep talking, fifteen years of my life were a waste of time …

The simplest thing is: if the fake gurus can fob you off with "intense sensations" as signs of spiritual progress, then a violent stomach ache after too much ice cream should be a reliable precursor to imminent enlightenment, right?

Oh my God, you're right! A sensation is a feeling, but it's far from being understanding and knowledge! But wasn't there any way for me to recognize such dead ends and to change course right away?

There is always a way, and that goes for all dead ends. But whether one is ready for it is directly proportional to the greed for the goods that a fake guru offers. The more a person craves deep feelings, recognition, appreciation, the feeling of "we", flattery, feelings of power, feelings of "being chosen", the harder it is to return to the light. We have already talked about this. The false pride of the gold miner. The exchange of goods between the perpetrator and the victim.

So that's why rescuing someone from the clutches of these traps and sects is so difficult. I usually managed to escape such brainwashing

sooner or later, but only when I myself decided to. Before that, warnings from whatever source just annoyed me.
Even today, many of my friends from back then are still victims of such manipulation. There wasn't a single case where I succeeded in getting them out of it. False pride and satisfaction with substitute drugs – you can't fight those.
By the way, what's your most successful strategy, in your experience? What is your most effective poison, to put it plainly? Perhaps then I'll be able to recognize which antidote works best.

Well, you have to be flexible! ***The most effective tool is always the one that works.*** Every person is different, everyone reacts differently to my traps, to my enticement to be led astray. But from a purely statistical point of view? That would be the drug "attention". For just an ounce of applause, appreciation, praise and flattery, you people are willing to swap a pound of freedom of thought, of movement, of love.

I just realized that was a silly question, because I could have come up with the answer myself, looking at my own past.

Correct. We should not ignore the best devil hack here, even if it is not so easy to apply:
Immunity to flattery. The strengthening of genuine self-sufficiency. And the reinforcement of a certain realization, namely that Buddy is always present and never lets anyone down.

Yes, and then I mustn't fail to mention another one of my strokes of genius, following on from the drug "attention" …

Not to do what really brings you joy until you "retire" is the surest way to forget what joy actually is and where it comes from. There is nothing left to fall back on. Like a bicycle whose rust weighs heavier than the other parts. It is not for nothing that the proverb says: "Perfect character is to live each day as if it were your last. Neither agitated nor tense nor unreal." (The Translator)

And what would that be?

Obedience. Or rather, the glorification of obedience as a virtue in itself. Without questioning to whom or what one is obedient, and what the consequences are, for the individual, for his country, for the world.

That strikes a chord with me as well. As a child of the 1950s and a teenager of the 1960s, I know exactly what you're talking about. Blind obedience! Yes, exactly! I realized early on what a powerful poison that is, and how many people's lives it has cost. At that time, of course, I first tried to be a "good" student, even in Sunday school with its badges for good behavior. Today I see, thanks also to this conversation with you, the perversity of an elementary school report card which only grades behavior & conduct, diligence and religion at the end of the school year. And only "A's" in these subjects were acceptable. A "B" meant you couldn't transition to the "Gymnasium", the exclusive German secondary school. We kids were so afraid of the teachers, and even more so of our parents - I still recall our efforts to get those "diligence testimonials". Disgraceful!

Right. The grade you got for behavior & conduct told how perfectly you would dance to the tune of authorities in the future. Best to leave your heart and brain behind at the gates of the school, the factory, the barracks. Later, the boss, supervisor, sergeant, leader, guru will be pleased with this ability. And the diligence grade is important because it says something about how well you can grit your teeth and persevere, no matter how sensible or senseless a task. And the grade for religion, of course, we've already discussed: you're confirming that you have assimilated the goods from the religion hawkers and then gradually turned them into something sacred and untouchable. The fact that the babble of a pope has been considered "infallible" since 1870, that was my work, yeah!

Oh man, you are an artist of darkness …

You bet I am. But for the sake of your peace of mind, you shouldn't overlook an important factor: the lives of those who demand blind obedience, senseless diligence and religious fanaticism are often doomed as well, because they have consecrated their minds to something fanatical and artificial at an early age – at the expense of their natural connection to Buddy. Those who demand obedience and, at the same time, the destruction of your moral compass, are seducers and tyrants. Their path leads straight into my arms.

No comfort from your words here. Recently I read a report about some parents whose twenty-one year old daughter was "disobedient". The young woman had disobeyed dad´s order to be home at a certain time. At twenty-one years old! As a punishment, her parents ordered her to kill her beloved dog. They drove outside of the city, and her father himself pressed the gun into her hand. Instead of killing the dog, the woman shot herself – in front of her parents. Obedience to the objective necessities of a situation, that's one thing, but blind obedience is pure poison.

And I've planted a trick in this matter.

Wouldn't surprise me anymore.

Look back at your youth and at yourself even sometimes today, then bring to mind all the people you know, privately, from the media, literature and politics, who resist blind obedience. They sometimes act not out of love, out of reason, out of morality, but out of childish *defiance*. If something is demanded of you, and you *automatically* do the opposite, you are just as dependent on the other person as if you always obeyed. In both cases – in blind obedience and in blind resistance – you are not the master of your actions but a robot. In both cases, you are mine.

Okay, enough now. What does the devil hack look like here?

I picked you because you and your readers would surely figure it out for yourselves. But I'll spell it out for you: ***before acting, switch on your heart and brain, and wait until you've finished thinking things through***.

Sorry, sometimes I tend to make things easy for myself.

Easier than necessary for real progress? Here I am!

A magic dwells in each beginning, protecting us, telling us how to live. High purposed we must traverse realm after realm, cleaving to none as to a home. The world spirit wishes not to fetter us, but to raise us higher, step by step. (Hermann Hesse)

OK let's have it …

To put it another way: one of my most cunning moves was to instill in people with good intentions the compulsion to please everyone – parents, teachers, professors, employers, superiors, even what you imagine Buddy wants from you. Those who feel this compulsion are not good people but compulsive people. By the way, they are often victims of exploitation.

I know this compulsion all too well. Saying "no" has never been one of my strengths. It's gradually getting better, though. By now, I can even complain to the waiter if the food was lousy. Yes, some people call "experience" what they've been doing wrong for forty years.

And here comes the appropriate devil hack:
Do right and fear no one.
Do only right by yourself and bear the consequences.
You will soon realize that this has nothing to do with egotism, quite the contrary. Only then will you be of real use to other people, because you will be able to judge much more accurately what is really helpful, and what is not. If you want to please an alcoholic and constantly supply him with alcohol "with good intentions", what

are you? If a woman has a violent partner, what exactly does it mean to "please" him just so he won't resort to violence? Acting like his doormat in the constant hope that he'll change for the better because, after all, he "doesn't really mean it"? Or are you being virtuous when you give him a *real* chance to get better by breaking up with him? Google the word "co-dependency" to get a handle on it. Here´s an old saying: "The road to hell is paved with good intentions." I didn't come up with that saying, though, because it's actually good for waking people up.

Hm, co-dependency … I know the word, but it's strange applying it to myself.

People are co-dependent when they support one another's addiction and dependency because *they can't help it,* because they are living in bondage, because they are victims of a helper syndrome. The partner's addiction may be to drugs, exercise of power, sex, attention, applause. The list is long. **As I said – if you can't help being good, you're bad.**

Fanatically standing up for good is not good, but fanaticism. Well, what you call "egotism" in everyday language is almost always a form of self-harm that isolates its victims.

Question: is there any element of our everyday life which you don't have a hand in? In other words: where we are solely responsible for ourselves?

Well, actually not, because one of my tasks is to make the wrong path feel pleasant to you everywhere. But since you're asking: what you made out of the term "honor" – well, I couldn't have done it better. It's similar to the "hurt feelings" issue. Honorable behavior, man, that used to be a mental bulwark against me! Today, in "defending honor", humans reach the heights of absurdity. You've killed people for burning a piece of cloth – for example, the flag of a country, of a soccer team or a family. You allow a brother to kill his sister because she was raped and therefore "dishonored the good name of the family". Or even worse, because she loved someone who followed a different religion than her family. Friend, everything a family does to whitewash its name dishonors the family a thousand times more than the original "offence"! You wage small and great wars for the sake of some imagined "honor". Characteristic phrase: "You can't do that to *me*!"

How could this happen? I have the feeling that it's gotten worse in recent decades. In the past, as a youngster, I liked to go to a soccer match now and then. Today, you can't go near the "Ultras", the most fanatic fans, with the "wrong" flag.

Originally, "honor" was a short term for the "dignity of the soul". It was invulnerable, nothing could harm it. In fact, nothing *can* harm it.
Today, however, you have turned the meaning upside down and into something closer to hot air than something of lasting value. Almost everything you do today to defend or even save 'honor" in fact amounts to an attack on the dignity of the soul. Hey, today, your dictionaries actually define "honor" as "social coercion"! That is correct! You have turned the real dignity of the soul into a clasp, a shackle, where what others think about you is a thousand times more important than what you think about yourself.
In short, "honor" has degenerated into a bogus concept which has been inflicted on you like a straitjacket. And what refugees and immigrants from macho and patriarchal countries carry with them with regard to their views of "honor", of course, reinforces this.
How to escape this? By thinking a bit about what one of my friends had to say recently: "My honor? If someone called me the biggest jerk on earth, I would never feel that my honor had been offended. Because there would be only two possibilities: he is not right, in which case I have no reason to get upset. Or he is right, in which case I have to be grateful to him because I made a mistake and can learn from it." Amen.

This reminds me of something Gandhi said: "If you are in the right, you can afford to be calm. If you are wrong, you cannot afford to lose your calm."

Yes, my friend, there's nothing new under the sun. You know everything, you have already heard and seen everything – now you just have to apply it …

Something occurs to me now, and I'm sure it will interest many readers: what about the Commandment "Honor thy father and thy mother"?

Devil Hacks

Life in itself is never anything, it is always only the favorable moment for something.
(Friedrich Hebbel)

Yes, yes, I have endeavored for millennia to get you to ignore something here, namely the second part of this commandment "… if they are worthy of honor." With my help, you have lost sight of the fact that free will gives you the freedom to look for your true family yourself here on earth. Biological parents are sometimes nothing more than a great test of your ability to get out of the way of what keeps you from your true calling.

"… if they are worthy of honor." – I wish more people would keep this truth in mind and dare to live by it. But I'm almost just talking to myself here.

True harmony within a family is a great blessing. But part of my job was to disguise the fact that being biologically related – whether as father or son, as mother or daughter, and so on – never automatically *entitles* you to anything! To maintain ties to biological relatives is important, but not in the way in which you have learned it. They are not a safe stronghold, they are not entitled to anything. The love of parents, the love of children, there is nothing "natural" or "self-evident", it doesn't come from the genes.

In their current lives, many souls have chosen exactly those parents, children, brothers and sisters to learn the proper way of relating to them, to form the relationships as a challenge to do the right thing, the human thing, the loving and positive thing for all involved. In some cases, however, this is only possible when one has finally realized that the *true* brothers and sisters, the *true* parents and children, live somewhere else entirely.

Strong stuff. When word gets out about this, many people will end up very lonely. And many others will finally be able set out to seek their true happiness, freed from taboos of thought and action. So the bottom line is: what can we do to escape your influence in the world? How can I help those around me? What's the ultimate devil hack against you?

I'll now hand you the most successful talisman against me. It is this:

Recognize the devil in your everyday life,
and then ignore him deliberately
and with full intention and determination.

Fighting me is the surest way to make me stronger. Whatever you turn your attention to, to that thing, that person or that situation, you give strength and keep it alive. That is why revolutions are almost never followed by an improvement in conditions. That which is opposed derives justification for its existence from the energy of the opponent. I know that this correlation is difficult for you to understand, but that does not alter its validity. Whatever you are fighting, you will strengthen. If your thoughts always revolve around the opponent, you constantly give the opponent the power and the right to exist.

I thank Buddy for allowing me the good fortune of knowing Him as the key to our true bliss. I never go to bed without considering that I might not be alive (as young as I am) anymore the next morning. And yet not one of all those who know me could say that I'm grumpy or sad in my dealings. And for this bliss and happiness I give thanks every day and wish it from the bottom of my heart to every one of my fellow men. (Mozart, letter to his father in 1787)

When you have awakened and realize clearly: "The situation I was born into, the family, the religion, the script that others wrote for me, that is not me!" When you have opened your eyes that wide, then you should not waste time justifying your longing for the far horizon but rather grow wings. Debating with prison guards does not open the gates of the prison.

We've already talked about this while on the subject of terrorism. One last devil hack, please? What can the world use as first aid measures to avoid disaster?

A short checklist, you mean? The list is really longer, of course, as all your readers who've made it this far will have realized, but for a start it would be great if you did the following:

* *As I said before: commit your children to travel around the world for a full year after school. On foot or by bike. Create an infrastructure for it, youth hostels everywhere; everywhere the possibility to work for a while, to keep a diary, to learn to listen, to build bridges between all people, all castes, all backgrounds. The generation that starts this off is the generation that will save you from yourselves.*

* *Introduce true pricing instead of subsidizing self-poisoning with your own taxes! Then, for example, organic food would be much cheaper than the normal junk you eat. Wood would be much cheaper than coal and oil. Renewable energy would be profitable. True-cost pricing would stop the destruction of the earth.*

* *You have to nationalize water and electricity supply services, thus putting it back in your own hands instead of letting a few exploit you all. Also nationalize all public transport and make it free of charge. You could afford it.*

* *Send one tenth of all military spending to those countries that are now sending you refugees, and closely control the use of that money. No one would have to flee from there anymore. Help people help themselves.*

* *And the little thing we've just been talking about: in functioning democracies no one should be allowed to post anonymously on the Internet. You should be able to identify who says what. You have to drain the hate.*

More than these simple measures would not be necessary to start with. Within just a few decades, the world would be transformed into a paradise for everyone.

Peace enters the soul of the people, Buddy is real, and we can find him even in this lifetime. Many prayers rise from the people's hearts: for money, fame, health and all sorts of other things. But the most insistent prayer of every heart should be for Buddy´s presence. Imperceptibly but surely, you will, of your own accord, arrive at the realization that Buddy is the only object of desire, the only goal that can satisfy you; for in Buddy lies the fulfilment of all the heart´s desires. Your soul is a temple of Buddy, and the darkness of human ignorance and earthly limitation must be driven out of this temple. It is wonderful to rest completely in the consciousness of the soul – strong and steadfast! Do not be afraid of anything! Hate no one, give your love to all, feel Buddy´s love, see him in every human being, and desire nothing but that he dwell constantly in the temple of your consciousness; that is the right way to live in this world. (Yogananda)

It sounds too good to be true … Just briefly, what exactly do you mean by "true-cost pricing"? I do know, but anyway, I'd like to hear your view.

Just consider any product, any human achievement, and imagine that, along the way to its realization, all those involved receive a decent reward for their effort, that allows them to live a decent and dignified life and to feed a family. Also imagine that their working conditions are decent and dignified, with health care. That all the costs of eliminating environmental damage and health impairments along the production process and subsequent recycling are included in the price of the product. Imagine that when trading the product or service, a fair price is achieved for all parties involved. If you could manage the economy with true-cost pricing, the earth would be a paradise.

And a fast food hamburger would probably cost ten times as much, wouldn't it?

Without a doubt. True-cost pricing would save you from yourselves. Unfortunately, the word hasn't gotten around to your economists, as you know.

Saving us from ourselves ... So our free market economy is ...

... liberating only for a small percentage of you.

That's probably the best criticism of capitalism I can imagine. All well and good, but what is our actual task as human beings which you're so keen to distract and divert us away from? What does Buddy have in mind for us? Could you put it in simple terms for my readers?

Time and again, Buddy wants to end the game of hide and seek that she herself started with each of you. She wants to find you, she wants to be found. And then everyone will burst into happy laughter together, because it was so much fun and so interesting, after all these adventures and experiences. Once again, even if almost everything seems to contradict it, the meaning of life is:

To get to know love, to give it and to receive it,
and to rejoice in it – in love and in life.
To beautify and improve what you come in contact with.
To learn ceaselessly what there is to learn,
and to pass on what you have learned with joy.

That would be the meaning of life, no more and no less. The path towards it – in the beginning the adventure, then the awareness of, then the direct experience of this truth – is not always discernible in everyday life. Not to believe in it seems easier, more plausible and sometimes even more pleasant than to hold fast to it and to make it the guiding star in one's life. This, however, is the first great test on this path.

Whoever recognizes that he has free will and the freedom to decide for himself has almost passed the test.

Suddenly I remember: I have a plane to catch! I glance at the big clock above the bar. The conversation must have lasted hours, but the clock shows 3:35 a.m. – my boarding has just started, there's still plenty of time. I turn to Fred – but he's disappeared.

"What gentleman?", the drowsy bartender replies when I ask him about Fred. He hasn't seen anyone around, he says, I've been his only guest for the past half hour …

I automatically touch the seat where Fred was sitting just a moment ago. It is warm …

I get up, stow away my little notebook and my cell phone with the recording – and I have a new task.

Dear reader,

Do you have a question for Fred?

AskFred@A1.net

Sorry, I don't know,

if you will receive an answer.

ABOUT THE AUTHOR

In 1991 Thomas Poppe published, together with Johanna Paungger, the runaway world bestseller "The Power of Timing" about the ancient knowledge of the influences of natural and lunar rhythms on everyday life.

Numerous other books by the author duo followed, heralding a renaissance in health awareness, and providing a myriad of practical tips for everyday life. Their work saw translation in 30 languages and more than 20 million copies sold in German alone.

In addition, they have developed a comprehensive calendar program that puts the insights of lunar knowledge into practice day by day.

With his books Thomas Poppe gives his readers useful and effective tools to create a better world. This is no different in "Espresso with the Devil".

Further English language books by Thomas Poppe

The Code

The Code introduces readers to an enriching and timeless tradition practiced for centuries in Western Europe. Going beyond simple numerology and mystic numbers, **The Code** offers a practical guide to discovering your personal tendencies, choosing a career, raising children, navigating relationships, and living a fulfilling, healthy life.

The basics: Each number in your birthdate has its own unique meaning and secret attributes that influence your abilities, personality, and relationships. By integrating the power of your birthday numbers with corresponding colors, the number wheel vividly shows you how to find balance and harmony, unearth your hidden talents, and navigate daily life.

For generations the number wheel has been used by the people of Tyrol to help raise children, choose a profession, treat illness, and make choices that promote physical and emotional well-being. The Code offers time-tested indigenous knowledge that has been effectively used for centuries.

The Power of Timing

(Wisdom Keeper Publications / Amazon)

The Essential Guide to Living in Blissful Harmony with Natural an Lunar Rhythms – A Landmark International Bestseller

You've probably always known that the moon's rhythms affect the world in certain ways - the ebb and flow of the tides, the most beneficial times to plant and harvest - but are you aware of its influence on virtually all the important areas of your daily life? If not, you're not alone. Effortless weight loss and control – without yo-yo effect * Speedy, scar free recovery after planned surgeries * Body care, beauty care and anti-aging the natural way * Effortless housekeeping with long-lasting effects * Green building and renovating with enduring results * Organic and sustainable gardening, farming and forestry with less toil, more fun and results to be proud of: The list of benefits does not stop here! In **The Power of Timing** the authors Johanna Paungger and Thomas Poppe reintroduce an ancient wisdom and give a straightforward promise: All of that list and more will happen if you start to apply a few basic principles of timing in your life. **The Power of Timing** will prove to be an invaluable resource in your quest to live a happier, more harmonious life. As part of a common inheritance it can move us a big step into a good future for us all.

Moon Time

(Rider / Random House London)

Direct perception and experience led our ancestors to the discovery that the success of many activities in daily life is subject to natural rhythms and the position and phases of the moon.

Moon Time shows:

* The way to a healthy life based on timeless knowledge that we have either forgotten or learned to ignore

* The influence of the moon and other natural rhythms on health and healing

* Healthy nourishment and living in harmony within the cycles of the moon

* The power of the mind

* The influence of all these aspects on body, mind and spirit.

Here is knowledge that will stay with you for life. This is the medical science of the future.